The Talking Cure

Marie-Louise von Franz, Honorary Patron

Studies in Jungian Psychology
by Jungian Analysts

Daryl Sharp, General Editor

THE TALKING CURE

Psychotherapy

Past, Present and Future

1

The Founding Fathers—
Sigmund Freud and C. G. Jung

ANTHONY STEVENS

Library and Archives Canada Cataloguing in Publication

Stevens, Anthony,1933-
  The talking cure : psychotherapy : past, present and future /
  Anthony Stevens / 3 volumes.

(Studies in Jungian psychology by Jungian analysts ; 136-138)

Includes bibliographical references and index.

ISBN 978-1-894574-38-9 (v. 1). —ISBN 978-1-894574-39-6 (v. 2).
—ISBN 978-1-894574-40-2 (v. 3)

  1. Psychotherapy. I. Stevens, Anthony, 1933-. II. Title. III. Series: Studies in
Jungian psychology by Jungian analysts ; 136.

RC480.S84 2012   616.89   C2012-904231-5

INNER CITY BOOKS

Box 1271, Station Q, Toronto, ON M4T 2P4, Canada.
Telephone (416) 927-0355 / Fax (416) 924-1814
Toll-free (Canada and U.S.): Tel. 1-888-927-0355 / Fax 1-888-924-1814
Web site: www.innercitybooks.net
E-mail: booksales@innercitybooks.net

Honorary Patron: Marie-Louise von Franz.
Publisher and General Editor: Daryl Sharp.
Associate Editor: Frith Luton.
Senior Editor: Victoria B. Cowan.
Office Manager: Scott Milligen.
Technical Support: David Sharp (www.sharpconnections.com)

INNER CITY BOOKS was founded in 1980 to promote the
understanding and practical application of the work of C. G. Jung.

Cover Image: Whorl of ancient ancestry.

Printed and bound in Canada by Thistle Printing Company Limited.

CONTENTS

THE TALKING CURE in three volumes

CONTENTS

CONTENTS

ACKNOWLEDGEMENTS

This book is the result of a professional lifetime spent in the practice of psychotherapy, and, inevitably, I have sometimes drawn on material previously written and published by me. I should, consequently, like to express my thanks to the Oxford University Press for permission to use material from my *Jung*, originally published in their Past Masters Series in 1993, and to Routledge for material from *Archetype: A Natural History of the Self* published in 1982 and from *Evolutionary Psychiatry: A New Beginning* written in collaboration with John Price and originally published in 1996, with a greatly revised edition in 2000. In addition, I must thank Routledge and the Princeton University Press for permission to quote from *The Collected Works of C. G. Jung*; Random House for permission to quote from *Memories, Dreams, Reflections* by C. G. Jung, recorded and edited by Aniela Jaffé; and the Hogarth Press for permission to quote from *Attachment and Loss: Volume 2, Separation: Anxiety and Anger*, by John Bowlby.

I should also like to thank all those friends, colleagues and patients, who have contributed to the thoughts and opinions presented in this book. I am particularly indebted to Dr Verena Kast, Dr Wolfram Keller, Dr Tom Kirsch, Dr Guido Mattanza, Dr Frank Margison, Professor David Orlinsky, Dr John Price, the late Professor Paul Roazen, Dr Seth Isaiah Rubin, Dr Mario Schlegel, the late Dr Anthony Storr, and Dr Margot Waddell for their valuable guidance and advice, and to Professors Paul Gilbert and Spencer Millham, and Andrew Samuels, who kindly read and commented on portions of earlier drafts. I hasten to add that none of these kind people should be taken to task for any of the views expressed in the chapters that follow—except where otherwise stated, these are my own and I accept full responsibility for them.

INTRODUCTION

Well over a century has elapsed since 'Anna O.', the patient so famously treated by Sigmund Freud's Viennese colleague Joseph Breuer, coined the term 'talking cure' for the treatment he gave her. Her case was destined to become the prototype of psychoanalytic cure, held up by Freud, and by generations of Freudian analysts, as the model of how a successful psychoanalysis should be conducted. We now know, however, that her treatment was not successful, and that the claims that Freud made for it were spurious. Anna's talking cure was no cure at all.

As a result of this and a number of other specious claims and instances of sharp practice that have come to light, Freud's reputation has been seriously compromised and the effectiveness of the whole psychoanalytic enterprise called into question. Inevitably, the contagion has spread to implicate other schools of analysis (the Jungian school being no exception) and has led to demands that the basic principles and practices of all forms of psychotherapy should be subjected to critical scrutiny and their therapeutic effectiveness (or otherwise) thoroughly assessed.

As the Freudian clinician and theoretician J.A. Arlow wrote with commendable foresight as long ago as 1982:

> We are approaching a post-apostolic era in psychoanalytic history. In a few years, we will no longer have with us colleagues who had direct or indirect contact with the founding fathers. Our confidence in our work will have to rely not on the memories of bygone heroes but on solid observational data, meticulously gathered in the analytic situation and objectively evaluated, for it is upon this set of procedures that the claim of psychoanalysis to a place among empirical sciences is based.

The 'post-apostolic era' is now well and truly upon us, and we have entered a new phase: the 'research and evidence-based revolution'. The very survival of different kinds of psychotherapy now depends on their ability to provide evidence proving that they regularly succeed in their therapeutic objectives, and do so at a cost that people (as well as government bodies and trusts) can reasonably afford.

This discipline is both salutary and beneficial in that it has generated carefully conducted research programs that have established beyond doubt that psychotherapy works. From its beginnings as a treatment for the privileged few, effective forms of psychotherapy have become widely available to large numbers of people suffering from a variety of mental health problems and personal crises.

However, there has been relatively little progress in developing an evidence base for longer-term psychodynamic therapies, such as those offered by Jungians and neo-Freudians. The extensive research of recent years has failed to establish that one form of therapy is any more effective than others across a range of psychological disorders. In other words, Jungian analysis has not been shown to produce better therapeutic outcomes than cognitive behaviour therapy or psychotherapeutic counselling. This finding has come to be known as the 'Dodo bird verdict' (after the Dodo bird in *Alice in Wonderland*, who, judging the outcome of a race, gave his verdict that 'Everyone has won and all must have prizes.').

For psychodynamic practitioners of psychotherapy the Dodo bird verdict has added to the crisis caused by the decline in the authority of Freud. It has meant that they have had to take a critical look at the principles and postulates on which their practices are based. It requires a detailed assessment of how these came into being, the extent to which their present use is therapeutically valid, what research can achieve in testing and improving them, and what may be done to guide them productively into the future.

The three slim volumes of this work are offered as a contribution to this vital self-monitoring process. They are intended not only for my professional colleagues and for those entering the profession as candidates, but also for members of the public who may be contemplating therapy for themselves. Essentially, I am asking three basic questions: where have we come from, where are we now, and where do we seem to be heading?

The Talking Cure in three volumes

Each volume addresses crucial stages in the development of psychoanalytic theory and practice. Inevitably, some readers will be more interested in one stage than the others and may not wish to acquire all three volumes. Accordingly, each volume is self-contained with its own glossary, bibliography and index. For those who prefer to follow the development of all three stages, all three volumes are designed to cohere in a logical sequence.

In presenting a critical assessment of the major schools of psychodynamic psychotherapy, their history and development up to the present time, I have been inspired by Jung's insight that every psychological system (his own included) is imbued with the personal psychology of its originator. As a result, chapters in each volume that deal with the emergence of different schools begin with a biographical account, showing how their theories and practices arose as direct expressions of their creators' 'personal equation'. Their contents are summarized below:

1: The Founding Fathers—Sigmund Freud and C. G. Jung

1. What Is Psychotherapy?
This section provides an overview of the different kinds of psychotherapy available, and summarizes their therapeutic principles. Research demonstrates that they are all effective. Since all are attempts to conceptualize the same phenomena it is not surprising that they influence one another. There are signs that they are becoming more integrated. The special case of psychoanalysis and its present uncertain status is discussed.

2. Psychoanalysis and Sigmund Freud (1856–1939)
Freud's life is examined to demonstrate his most salient qualities: his intellectual brilliance, his obsessive dedication to hard work, his outstanding gifts as a writer and extempore lecturer, his virtuoso ability to play with ideas and juggle them into new syntheses, his intolerance of criticism or dissent, his overriding ambition and his single-minded determination to succeed. Freud's most extraordinary achievements were neither clinical nor scientific but personal and promotional. With impressive tactical skill he was able to present himself as a fearless searcher after truth, totally incapable of fraud or malpractice. Now that this self-serving myth has been torn away, he stands exposed as an unscrupulous clinician, capable of bullying his patients into providing the data he

needed to 'prove' his aetiological fantasies, and of generating an extensive literature that recycled a tiny number of 'classic' cases with such consummate cunning as to create the illusion of an enormous clinical database.

Yet, for all that, Freud remains an outstanding historical figure, more famous by far than any of his critics or detractors. How did he do it? The development of his theories is described and their extraordinary cultural impact, analysed.

3. Analytical Psychology and Carl Gustav Jung (1875–1961)

More than any other psychologist, Jung's understanding of humanity grew directly out of his understanding of himself. From childhood he possessed a genius for introspection that enabled him to attend closely to experiences proceeding on or below the threshold of consciousness—experiences of which most people are unaware. This chapter describes how the main innovations that Jung introduced into psychotherapy arose out of the 'creative illness' (he called it his 'confrontation with the unconscious') that he suffered after the disintegration of his deeply ambivalent friendship with Freud. As Jung emerged from a near psychotic state, he recognized two personalities in himself (No. 1 and No. 2, which he later identified respectively, with the ego and the Self) and proceeded to formulate his ideas concerning the collective unconscious, archetype, complex, shadow, persona, animus, anima, psychological types, and the individuation of the Self. In his therapeutic practice Jung reacted strongly against the stereotype of the classical Freudian analyst, sitting aloof and silent behind the recumbent patient on the couch, occasionally emitting *ex cathedra* pronouncements and interpretations while remaining uninvolved in the patient's anxieties and sufferings. Abandoning the use of the couch, Jung offered the radical proposal that analysis is a *dialectical procedure,* a two-way exchange between two people, who are equally involved—a model that has come to influence psychotherapists of most schools, though many seem not to realize that it originated with Jung.

This chapter examines Jung's views on the practice of analytical psychology, the interpretation of dreams, the amplification of symbols, the mobilization of unlived potential in the Self, and his therapeutic use of the biological principles of adaptation, homeostasis and epigenesis to activate the psyche's capacity to heal itself.

2: Warring Egos, Object Relations and Attachment Theory

1. Ego Psychology and the Analysis of Children

Child analysis was pioneered by Anna Freud (1895–1982) and Melanie Klein (1882–1960). They hated one another and their mutual hostility divided the British psychoanalytic movement into two, eventually three, antagonistic groups. Anna was highly gifted but never really grew up, remaining her 'father's daughter' all her life. Freud trained her as a 'lay' analyst and analysed her himself, a case of 'psychological incest' they managed to keep secret for many years. Anna, who never married, had a close relationship with Dorothy Burlingham, whose children she analysed. She published *An Introduction to the Technique of Child Analysis* in 1927 and the influential *The Ego and the Mechanisms of Defence* in 1936 as an 80th birthday present for her father. Extending Freud's topographical model (published in his *The Ego and the Id* in 1923), Anna maintained that ego defences could be adaptive as well as pathological and that their analysis required tact and a strong therapeutic alliance. The importance of Heinz Hartmann (1894–1970) is acknowledged. He sought to put Anna's work on an evolutionary basis, arguing that children are designed by natural selection to be adapted to their surroundings, thus anticipating the work of John Bowlby (1907–1990) and contemporary evolutionary psychologists. In contrast to Freud's emphasis on the father, Anna stressed the importance of the mother, arguing that child development depended less on instinctual repression than on attachment to the adults caring for them. She inaugurated the systematic observation of children and the use of research programs to test and develop psychoanalytic theories.

That dysfunctional families tend to produce dysfunctional families was certainly true of Melanie Klein's family history. To this can be attributed her lifelong preoccupation with the dominant issues of unrequited love, anger, envy, anxiety and despair. Being the victim of a domineering, manipulative mother, a neglectful father, a series of traumatic bereavements, and recurrent bouts of depression meant that she never achieved a satisfactory emotional or sexual relationship, was an inadequate mother to her three children, and provoked strongly ambivalent feelings in everyone she encountered. Alone among her siblings, she was not breast-fed by her mother which may account for the theoretical emphasis she placed on the child's relationship with its mother's breast.

To find some relief from her problems, she started reading Freud and went into analysis with Sándor Ferenzci (1873–1933) in Budapest in 1913 and later with Karl Abraham (1877–1925) in Berlin, both of whom encouraged her to specialize in the analysis of children. Impressed by her work, Ernest Jones, Director of the British Psychoanalytic Institute, invited her to England. She took London by storm, quickly polarizing opinion between those analysts who accepted her ideas about primitive infantile experiences and those who did not. The split, which was essentially about personalities, lasted the rest of the century. All Klein's revisions of psychoanalytic theory and practice (which are examined in this chapter) were systematically rejected by Anna Freud. For all their mutual loathing, both Melanie Klein and Anna Freud succeeded in making the mother and 'object relations' as central to psychoanalytic theorizing as Freud had made the father and sexual conflict.

2. Object Relations Theory

Though Melanie Klein prepared the path that led from Freudian Ego Psychology to modern object relations theories, she viewed the growing child's primary objective as striving to preserve its sanity by dealing with the psychotic terrors by which it was afflicted. It was this 'Hammer Studios' portrayal of life that the British object relations theorists were to modify. The main figures involved in these developments were Ronald Fairbairn (1889–1964), Donald Winnicott (1896–1971), Michael Balint (1896–1970), Harry Guntrip (1901–1974) and, most importantly, John Bowlby (1907–1990), who went on to develop his own Attachment Theory. Together they constituted what came to be known as the 'independent group' of psychoanalysts who, fed up with the implacable antagonism between Freudian and Kleinian factions, decided to go their own way in the spirit of 'a plague on both their houses'.

Each of them developed his own theoretical orientation, and their contributions are reviewed in the present chapter. Together they introduced a more balanced, and ultimately verifiable, conception of human development. These innovations were, however, richly dependent on their own psychology (their 'personal equation') as this chapter makes clear.

3. Attachment Theory: John Bowlby (1907–1990)
Bowlby was one of the most creative and influential psychiatrists produced by any nation in the twentieth century. Not only did he revolutionize psychoanalytic theory and transform our understanding of psychopathology, but he also provided a scientific basis for the practice of psychotherapy and improved the lot of children in hospitals and institutions throughout the world. This chapter examines Bowlby's contribution in detail, particularly his preoccupation with the key issues of *attachment, separation* and *loss*—a preoccupation that was a direct outgrowth of his own life experience.

3: The Way Ahead—Jung and Evolutionary Psychotherapy

1. Jung Revisited: The Personal Equation
Since the first two volumes have stressed the importance of personal factors in shaping what psychoanalysts write, it is only fair that I should say something about my own 'personal equation'. This chapter begins by describing my own engagement with Jungian Psychology; my analysis with Irene Champernowne (1901–1976); my training in psychology, medicine and psychiatry; my research on attachment behaviour in children in a Greek orphanage (with John Bowlby as my supervisor); and my eventual emergence as a Jungian analyst. While giving strong support to Bowlby's attachment theory, I realized, in the course of my Greek research, that by overlooking the archetypal background to the mother–child bond Bowlby excluded a dimension of enormous prognostic significance, for what matters more than the personal mother's behaviour is the *archetypal experience of mothering* activated by her in the child.

This realization is of enormous importance in the treatment of people with dysfunctional parental complexes, because those archetypal experiences the personal parents may fail to activate in the child persist nevertheless as *potential* in the child's unconscious psyche and seek actualization in reality. This insight represents a major advance on object

15

relations and attachment theories in understanding the creative significance of the transference and how it can be a determining factor in the
successful therapy of patients coming into analysis, as many do, with
'parent hunger'. This chapter also examines the contribution that Michael
Fordham (1905–95) made to the establishment of Jungian psychotherapy
in Britain and the United States. Founding the Society for Analytical
Psychology in 1946, Fordham saw himself as an innovator who corrected
deficiencies in Jung's theoretical legacy by stressing the importance of
transference interpretations and analysing the influence of infantile wishes and fantasies in personality development. His advocacy of a rapprochement between Jungian theories and those of neo-Freudian,
Kleinian and object relations schools, with a return to the use of the
couch and of reductive analysis, led to accusations that he had betrayed
the creative-symbolical approach of classical Jungian therapy, and resulted in the setting up of alternative Jungian training institutes. Thus,
Fordham's attempt to heal the split between Freud and Jung succeeded in
creating further splits within the Jungian camp in England and the U.S.

I describe my attempts to transcend these divisions in my *Archetype:
A Natural History of the Self* (1982) and *Archetype Revisited: An Updated Natural History of the Self* (2003), stressing the evolutionary implications of archetypal theory and the profound clinical and theoretical
importance of Jung's concept of the Self, not as something created afresh
by each individual in the course of personal development as the object
relations theorists believed, but as an inherent propensity—a 'given' responsible for guiding the personality in its development through the stages of life. Though Jungians have so far proved reluctant to explore the
rich avenue of possibilities that this approach opens up, it is nevertheless
being adopted by the new breed of evolutionary psychotherapists. I argue
that their work needs to be done in the spirit of Jung's broad humanity
and open-mindedness, and his understanding of the healing potentials
inherent in the Self.

2. Research

Research showing that elaborate long-term analysis is not indispensable
to favourable outcome threatens the very survival of traditional forms of
analytic therapy. This chapter presents the evidence and gives critical

16

examination to the Dodo bird verdict, arguing that the use of 'meta-analysis' to homogenise the results of thousands of different studies with hundreds of different client groups is inevitably going to obscure important differences between them. Meta-analysis served its purpose in demonstrating that all forms of psychotherapy work, but what researchers are increasingly having to examine is the issue of what works best for whom. The crucial questions for research to address were asked as long ago as 1967 by Gordon Paul: '*What* treatment, by *whom*', he wrote, 'is most effective for *this* individual with *that* specific problem, and under *which* set of circumstances?' Researchers are refining their techniques and some of Paul's questions are being answered, but there is still much ground to be covered. Features contributing to favourable outcome common to all therapies are increasingly understood and are carefully summarized. What research has great difficulty in assessing is the quality of the exchanges that occur in an analytic session: here the line between science and art grows hazy.

3. Evolutionary Psychotherapy

The views of different schools on the causes and treatment of psychological disorders are summarized and compared with the views current among evolutionary psychiatrists and psychotherapists. This chapter presents a crash course in evolutionary psychiatry, revealing its close compatibility with Jungian theory. Evolutionary psychiatry maintains that evolution has equipped us with a large repertoire of genetically encoded psychological mechanisms (Jung's archetypes of the collective unconscious) which enable us to respond adaptively to social and physical environmental events. Symptoms are not seen as signs of 'disease' but natural responses that can become distorted or exaggerated in response to contemporary environmental pressures, or as the result of 'the frustration of archetypal intent'.

Symptoms are thus richly meaningful adaptations. The evolutionary history and the selective advantages of anxiety, phobia, mania and depression are described and their psychopathology and treatment in contemporary patients, explained. In Jungian terms, these disorders provide examples of an archetype entering the personal psyche as a complex. To suffer from a phobia is to experience what it is to be in the grip of an 'autonomous complex'. A new classification of the major psychiatric disorders emerges. The 'biosocial goals' listed by evolutionary psychologists correspond neatly to the foci of interest of the main schools of analysis. The objections to applying Darwinian insights to human psychology are sympathetically examined, and shown to be mistaken.

Whatever upheavals may be in store for us as a result of theoretical revisions, outcome studies, clinical audits, and research on the biochemistry of the brain, the primary duty of the psychotherapist will remain the same: to put empathy, knowledge and professional skill at the service of the patient. To adopt an evolutionary approach is not to espouse a political cause, to submit to biological determinism or to abandon a proper concern for ethical values. What such an approach does provide is a compass and a new orientation to steer us through the immense complexities of human psychology, its disorders and their treatment.

1
WHAT IS PSYCHOTHERAPY?

It is a truth universally acknowledged that an unhappy person in possession of a good fortune must be in want of a psychoanalyst. That, at any rate, is the *New Yorker*'s view of the matter: the cartoon patient invariably ends up in a sparsely furnished study with a framed diploma on the wall, 'free associating' on a couch, at the head of which sits a bearded man with a bewildered expression on his face and a note pad on his knee—the classic psychoanalytic situation.

To most people terms like *psychologist, psychiatrist, psychoanalyst, Freudian* and *psychotherapist* are virtually synonymous, but to the specialist they mean very different things, and it will be helpful to be aware of these distinctions. A *psychologist* is a pure scientist who studies all behaviour, whether normal or abnormal, human or animal; a *psychiatrist* is a medically qualified practitioner who specializes in the treatment of all mental disorders, using drugs as well as psychological and social means; a *psychoanalyst* is a professional (who may or may not be medically qualified) who specializes in treating carefully selected patients using the theories and techniques devised by Sigmund Freud and his followers; while a *psychotherapist* may belong to any one of more than 400 different 'schools' of therapy, each with its own theoretical and methodological approach to the psychological treatment of people.

That all these different disciplines should be parcelled together in the common imagination and labelled 'psychoanalysis' bears eloquent testimony to the fame attained by Freud in his lifetime and maintained since his death. This is precisely as he would have wished it, for, as we shall see, he was a man driven by a single-minded determination to achieve professional distinction at all costs. It is not an exaggeration to say that psychoanalysis, and the many psychotherapeutic branches that grew off the original Freudian shoot, became a major manifestation of twentieth century cultural life—'the central imagination of our age', as Harold Bloom, the literary critic, called it. What started as an esoteric movement among a small central European clique was to become a growth industry which later threatened to run out of control, as more and more people presented themselves for treatment, and more and more prospective therapists sought to be trained or set themselves up in practice without any training at all.

The flowering of new therapeutic methods, based as they usually were on the theoretical assumptions of the charismatic figures who founded them (rather than on sound empirical evidence of their efficacy), grew into mutually exclusive 'sects', prone to entertain uncharitable and somewhat paranoid feelings about one another. In response to pressure from the European Union, efforts have been made in Great Britain to define the various therapies available and to establish their professional and legal status. These endeavours have been co-ordinated by the United Kingdom Council for Psychotherapy and the British Psychoanalytic Council which, as may be imagined, have had to referee battles which at times assumed such bitterness as to make Waterloo and Gettysburg resemble scuffles on a village green.

So *psychotherapy* cannot be regarded as a single entity: it is a term that covers a wide range of therapeutic philosophies or 'cultures', some of which retain the psychoanalytic model of unconscious motivation and the analysis of significant experiences from the patient's childhood or infancy, while others focus on the patient's conscious experience and behaviour in the here and now. However, all psychotherapists of whatever school broadly agree with the view that psychotherapy is an interpersonal process involving some form of contract between a trained professional and a patient, which is designed to bring about change in the ideas, feelings, attitudes and behaviour which have proved troublesome to the person seeking help.

What, then, are the main forms of therapy on offer? For the sake of clarity they may be broadly classified and briefly described under six headings (Parry, 1996; Roth and Fonagy, 2005):

> Psychoanalytic and psychodynamic therapies
> Behaviour and cognitive therapies
> Humanistic and existential therapies
> Family therapy
> Group therapy
> Counselling

I will look at these one by one.

Psychoanalytic and psychodynamic therapies
Both these forms of therapy are designed to enable patients to gain insight into their conscious and unconscious motives so as to resolve the conflicts considered responsible for their personal difficulties. The distinctions between the two forms of therapy are becoming blurred, but they mainly reflect differences in the intensity and timescale of the treatment program: psychoanalysis requires patients to attend three to five times a week and is open-ended; psychodynamic therapy requires one or two sessions a week and treatment is often limited to an agreed and pre-set period of time. The majority of practitioners of both kinds of therapy adhere to Freudian, neo-Freudian or Kleinian models of psychopathology and treatment. The minority adhere to a Jungian model.

The 'cathartic' approach, originally developed by Freud in collaboration with the Viennese physician Joseph Breuer, advocated a fairly brief form of therapy intended to do no more than remove 'hysterical' symptoms. Classical psychoanalysis, as Freud later developed it, became a longer, more intensive treatment designed not only to eliminate symptoms but also to bring about fundamental changes in the personality of the patient. Whether this objective was ever satisfactorily achieved is now open to debate; it nevertheless remains an acknowledged goal of psychoanalytic treatment.

In Britain, until the outbreak of the Second World War, psychoanalysis, whether Freudian, Kleinian or Jungian, was virtually the only form of psychological treatment available and, of necessity, was confined to a small patient population. The [Freudian] Institute of Psycho-Analysis was founded in 1919, the [at first Freudian but later Kleinian] Tavistock Clinic in 1920, the [Jungian] Society of Analytical Psychology in 1936 and the Anna Freud Centre in 1952. Analysis did not become available for patients under the National Health Service until 1948, and was effectively restricted to those living in the London area. Since then the cost-effectiveness of analytic treatment has increasingly become an issue, and the emergence of briefer, more focused types of psychodynamic therapy has been in part due to the uncertain results of classical psychoanalysis but most of all to the excessive time and expenditure involved.

Behaviour and cognitive therapies

Behaviour therapy was developed in Britain during the 1950s and 60s at the Maudsley Hospital and the Institute of Psychiatry in London. It was derived from classical learning theory and from conditioning experiments conducted on animals. Patients were treated for a variety of conditions, such as phobias, obsessive-compulsive disorders and alcoholism, by such techniques as negative reinforcement, desensitization, 'flooding' and response-inhibition.

True to the tenets of academic behaviourism, symptomatic 'responses' were the focus of therapeutic attention, and cognitive processes were ignored as irrelevant. By the 1970s, behavioural treatments were widely available under the NHS, mostly administered by clinical psychologists, many of whom had abandoned their ancillary role (as technicians applying diagnostic tests) in order to participate actively in the treatment of patients.

However, by the late 1960s, academic psychologists began to liberate themselves from the yoke of behaviourism and to acknowledge that people actually had minds to think with. This was the so-called 'cognitive revolution'. As a result, behaviour therapists started to take account of the cognitive processes occurring in their patients. Reluctantly at first, they came to share certain assumptions with psychodynamic therapists, namely, that the cognitive processes involved in symptom-formation may be unconscious as well as conscious, and that people can be self-destructive because of negative convictions about themselves, the world and the future. Such negative cognitions are understood to have developed through learning and to be maintained by reinforcement; and cognitive therapy aims to change these through a range of therapeutic techniques, such as identifying and challenging negative assumptions and encouraging patients to monitor their responses in the light of what they have learned in the therapeutic situation. Here again the influence of psychodynamic therapy is apparent.

Humanistic and existential therapies

Until the 1970s patients had a choice, when they had a choice at all, between submitting to psychoanalytic therapy on the one hand or behavioural therapy on the other. The gap between these two approaches was filled by the rapid emergence of new therapies based on the humanistic, existential and phenomenological ideas of Nietzsche, Sartre and Husserl. These ideas were taken up by clinicians such as Abraham Maslow, Fritz Perls, Carl Rogers and Eric Berne, who were part of what came to be known as the 'human potential movement'. Treatment was mainly available privately, though Carl Rogers' 'client-centred counselling' was used in some NHS services in England.

All these approaches eschew the 'deterministic-explanatory' model of psychodynamic therapies, maintaining that emotional problems arise when individuals are inhibited by social circumstances from actualizing their full potential. Instead of 'insight' or the removal of symptoms, 'clients' are helped to develop self-awareness while working towards the goal of self-determination. Therapists attempt to facilitate change through 'unconditional regard' for their clients, being open and receptive to their communications, and empathizing with their feelings. Initially, humanistic therapists maintained that it was their role to provide clients with a series of growth experiences rather than with treatment *per se*, stressing the importance of the therapist's attitudes rather than the use of therapeutic techniques. Gradually, however, specific techniques began to merge in such forms as psychodrama, role playing and various kinds of abreaction (discharge of emotions).

Though apparently very different from psychoanalytic therapies, there is an evident overlap between the humanistic approach and certain fundamental concepts of Jungian analysis, namely the idea that patients are in part suffering the consequences of unactualized psychic potential, that psychic development does not reach its peak in early adulthood but continues through the course of the entire life cycle, and that the goal of life is *individuation*—to become as whole and as complete a human being as one's circumstances allow.

Family therapy

As with humanistic therapies, this approach concerns itself less with symptom-removal or with insight into personal psychodynamics but more with the social system responsible for the patient's difficulties. This 'systemic' approach is derived from the science of cybernetics, with its concepts of homeostatic equilibrium, and positive and negative feedback.

While it can be used in analysing a number of social situations, it has found its most fruitful application in treating members of families. Each member is considered as a unit within the family system, and the task of therapy is to examine the strategic role that the patient's problem has been playing within the context of that system. Having identified this role, family therapists place emphasis on the positive and negative contributions that the patient's symptoms are making to the family system as a whole, and use advice, suggestion and the re-definition of boundaries between family members in order to render the system less dysfunctional. Although psychodynamic formulations are not encouraged, they nevertheless have a tendency to intrude into family therapy sessions, providing further evidence of the pervasive influence of psychoanalytic ideas.

Group therapy

This approach came into prominence during the Second World War when understaffed military hospitals were forced to use group treatment to deal with large numbers of psychiatric casualties. Though initially rooted in psychoanalytic concepts, group therapy rapidly became an eclectic procedure, transcending different theoretical orientations. It was enthusiastically adopted in the 1960s by the community mental health movement in the United States, with the subsequent development of short-term therapies designed to deal with here-and-now interpersonal problems, to promote self-awareness, reduce emotional dependency and enhance social competence. In both Britain and the United States, this coincided with the emergence of such 'movements' as the therapeutic community movement, the encounter group movement, group applications of transactional analysis, Esalen and EST.

Counselling

Counsellors, like psychotherapists, are people possessing varying degrees of competence, experience and training, and it is difficult to make hard and fast distinctions between them. On the whole, counsellors tend to work with people on their problems in dealing with the practical issues of life rather than attempting to treat their mental or emotional disturbances. While this constraint looks workable in theory, it is often difficult to sustain in practice, and counsellors, not infrequently, find themselves struggling to cope with psychiatric disorders which they are not adequately qualified to treat. Moreover, a complication arises when psychotherapists are euphemistically referred to as 'counsellors', especially within the NHS, where it is believed that general practice patients will find the idea of consulting a counsellor less of a social stigma.

A degree of overlap

While these six groups represent the main psychotherapeutic orientations discernible at the present time, there is, inevitably, some degree of overlap between them. In some instances this congruence has been exploited to develop new 'integrative therapies', such as the 'cognitive analytic therapy' of Anthony Ryle, which provides a structure in which to make a precise formulation of patients' problems in terms of their characteristic modes of relationship. Ryle's combination of cognitive and psychodynamic elements not only attracted new candidates for training but stimulated the interest of practitioners of both approaches. Since all psychotherapeutic orientations are attempts to conceptualize the same phenomena, it is understandable that they should influence one another; and research in the form of outcome studies designed to determine 'what works for whom' may serve to promote greater integration between all schools of therapy in the future. Should this be so, it will help to compensate in some measure for the serious decline in respect for psychoanalysis—and all forms of psychodynamic theory derived from it—which has resulted from the intellectual shipwreck of their founding father, Sigmund Freud.

The present status of psychoanalysis

Everyone has heard of Freud: his books and papers are the most cited by any author in twentieth-century literature. His influence, as we have already noted, has not only pervaded the practice of psychological therapies but has also entered the very fabric of our culture. In W. H. Auden's words, 'To us he is no more a person/ Now but a whole climate of opinion.' The idea that personality is the product of early childhood events, that human actions are unconsciously motivated, that a fulfilled sex life is crucial for human happiness, and that we tend to repress or

25

deny frightening or disagreeable facts, are notions that have come to be generally accepted as self-evident truths, yet they are largely products of Freud's inventive and persuasive genius.

As will become clear in the chapters that follow, analytic theories are speculative and deeply subjective phenomena, imbued with the psychology and professional ambitions of their originators. Consequently, the history of psychodynamic therapy has been stormy and dramatic—one of great personal achievements, intense political rivalries, inflammatory rhetoric between warring factions; and the emergence of independent 'schools', Jungians, Kleinians, Adlerians, Lacanians, Ego Psychologists, Object Relations Theorists, Self Psychologists and so on, each tending to have its own constitution, bureaucratic organization, official doctrine, specialist journals, initiation rituals and exclusive membership lists. Since there is little scientific evidence to justify such diversity, these different groups have been compared to religious sects or Athenean schools of philosophy.

Yet despite this proliferation, and the elaborate modifications psychoanalytic formulations have undergone, Freud remains a pivotal figure, a central reference point for all discussions and developments in psychodynamic discourse. This is unfortunate, for, as we shall see, Freud's scientific notions were already out of date when his psychoanalytic thinking began, and the evidence he produced to underpin his theoretical propositions was not infrequently of his own invention. Recognition of these facts brought about a radical reassessment of Freud's reputation.

Whereas for the greater part of the twentieth century informed opinion was sympathetic to Freud, this is no longer the case. Increasingly, attitudes hardened against him, and many came to share Sir Peter Medawar's bleak view of psychoanalysis as 'the most stupendous intellectual confidence trick of the twentieth century'. Telling indictments have come off the presses with increasing frequency: Frederick Crews's devastating articles in the *New York Review of Books* in 1993 and 1994, Allen Esterson's *Seductive Mirage: An Exploration of the Work of Sigmund Freud* (1993), Robin Tolmach Lakoff and James C. Coyne's *Father Knows Best: The Use and Abuse of Power in Freud's Case of "Dora"* (1993), Jeffrey Masson's *Against Therapy: Emotional Tyranny and the Myth of Psychological Healing* (1988, revised edition 1990), Richard Webster's

Why Freud Was Wrong (1995), Malcolm Macmillan's *Freud Evaluated* (1997) and Robert Wilcocks's *Maelzel's Chess Player: Sigmund Freud and the Rhetoric of Deceit* (1994)—these and others contributed to the landslide decline in Freud's scientific status and effectively diminished respect for all schools of dynamic psycho-therapy. This struck a note of alarm throughout the profession: for, if Freudian theory was without foundation, what was to stop the whole psychotherapeutic edifice from collapsing into the quicksands on which it was built?

Nor did that other charismatic figure, C. G. Jung, prove immune to attack. Although attempts to convict him of Nazi anti-semitic sympathies were discredited, Richard Noll's *The Jung Cult: Origins of a Charismatic Movement* (1994) and *The Aryan Christ: The Secret Life of Carl Jung* (1997) were widely noticed and praised. Noll accused Jung's followers of establishing 'an institutionalized capitalist enterprise' with training institutes and local psychology clubs distributed throughout the world. Jungian psychology, Noll argued, is a 'secret church', a religious cult, centred on the 'pseudo-charismatic' figure of Jung, and run by an elitist group of acolytes, who sold initiation into the 'fantasy of individuation' at an exorbitant price. Moreover, Noll tried to prove that Jungian psychology shared precisely the same Germanic, Aryan, 'völkisch', Nietzschean, sun-worshipping roots as National Socialism—though Noll acknowledged that Jung put this tradition to the service of 'religious' rather than political ends. While this is a biased and largely refutable examination of the shadow side of Jungian practice, as I showed in the second edition of my *On Jung* (1999), it fitted well with a growing prejudice against psychotherapy which saw it as a dubious activity—as snake-oil pedalled by hucksters.

The most serious charge made against psychoanalysis was not just that it is protracted and very expensive but that it is ineffective, in that it does not bring about the radical improvements that its practitioners claim. This is an issue that can only be decided by painstaking research, but research has been slow in coming, and the results have not been encouraging. Consequently, psychoanalysis now finds itself in a perilous position. From being the authoritative father of the psychotherapeutic movement, it has become its problem child. Since there is little or no research evidence to support the view that psychoanalysis brings about more radical or lasting improvements than other less expensive forms of psychotherapy (though the absence of evidence does not necessarily mean that it does not produce such improvements) and, since its theoretical foundations have been exposed as less than sound, many critics have argued that the entire psychoanalytic edifice should be pulled down and the site cleared for redevelopment. Others maintain that such drastic action is impractical because psychoanalytic thinking has become deeply enmeshed in our culture and extensively implicated in all psychotherapeutic practices. We have no alternative, they argue, than to assess what, if anything, is of lasting value in the psychoanalytic tradition and build on it, while calling in the bulldozers to get rid of those parts of the structure which are evidently jerry-built or have already collapsed.

Nevertheless, it is important to stress that the profession of psychotherapy will survive because there exist in our society so many people in distress, having major difficulties in their lives, who need the help of someone sympathetic to listen to their troubles and enable them to sort them out. The anxiety, self-doubt and despair that large numbers of people carry is very real, and the help that psychotherapy can provide is no less real, as much careful research has demonstrated. There is nothing wrong with the one-to-one therapeutic relationship as a procedure; what is defective is the theoretical context within which much psychotherapy is practised. And since theoretical considerations are of central significance in psychodynamic therapy—my own particular area of concern—they will feature largely throughout the course of this and subsequent volumes of this book.

The problem is that, if we abandon psychoanalytic theory altogether, psychodynamic therapists are left with no unitary, integrative paradigm in terms of which to make interpretations, propose hypotheses or proceed with any confidence in their work. Research then becomes entirely focused on 'outcomes' while saying nothing about the theoretical basis of the procedures whose outcomes are being measured. The solution to this predicament must surely be to replace psychoanalytic theories with a new paradigm. Does this new paradigm exist? I believe it does, as I hope to demonstrate in Volume 3.

Before it is possible to appreciate the explanatory value of the new paradigm, however, we must first examine the history of the old one.

Since people reading this book may be planning to train as psychotherapists, or may well be contemplating psychotherapy for themselves, the historical overview which follows should help them to appreciate what they may be letting themselves in for.

Caveat emptor!

2
PSYCHOANALYSIS AND SIGMUND FREUD (1856-1939)

Though Freud is rightly credited with the creation of psychoanalysis, the therapeutic relationship as a one-to-one interaction between a healer and a patient is a great deal older: we cannot know precisely when it began because its origins are shrouded in the mists of prehistoric time. As a species, we evolved in circumstances of great vulnerability, threatened by predators, natural disasters, hostile neighbours, malevolent spirits, diseases and death. It is not surprising that in such conditions a figure should emerge, whom anthropologists have detected in human settlements throughout the world, whose function it is to heal the infirm and bring comfort to those who are frightened, depressed, ill or sick at heart. The ubiquitous presence of the healer, priest, shaman, guru or witch doctor, and the practices and rituals of healing, are among the most striking of all cultural universals; and it is from these primordial roots that modern medicine, psychiatry and psychotherapy have grown.

The art of healing

What have patients always wanted of their healers? The ethnographic evidence points to four main requirements—the healer should:

(1) possess authority and charisma

(2) provide personal attention so that patients are given time for the nature of their complaints to be understood

(3) possess knowledge—a corpus of theory and practice from which a diagnosis, an explanation and appropriate treatment can be derived

(4) possess the ability to restore patients to health and to full participation in the community.

This still provides a good summary of what is expected of psychotherapists at the present time. A broad consensus also exists across a large number of different cultures concerning ideas about the cause of diseases and the best means of treating them. Two basic theories of pathology are apparent: (a) the idea that something has got out of the patient which ought to be there, and (b) that something has got into the patient which ought not to be there. Each of these theories is linked with an appropriate principle of treatment: if something has got out, replace it; if something has got in, remove it.

Patients who are ill because 'something has got out' are usually considered to have lost that ghostly entity which in our culture we call the soul; the function of the healer is to track down the errant soul and restore it to its rightful owner. Clinical descriptions of people considered to be suffering from loss of soul reveal a condition closely akin to what we diagnose as 'depression' or bereavement following the loss of someone beloved. The sufferer feels that something indispensable is missing; recovery is experienced when the vital spark of life returns. In *Modern Man in Search of a Soul* (1933) Jung diagnosed our whole culture as suffering from loss of soul. As we shall see, he believed he cured the condition in himself through what he called his 'confrontation with the unconscious', a form of shamanic initiation from which he was to derive the theory and practice of what has come to be known as *analytical psychology* (to distinguish it from Freud's *psychoanalysis*).

More commonly, illness is regarded as an evil intruder, an alien force or demon that has taken possession of the patient. Healing consists of excising or exorcising it. Among the Nepalese, for example, the healer will suck the illness from a patient and spit out something, which on subsequent examination proves to be a piece of animal or vegetable tissue. In the Philippines, so-called psychic surgeons carry out 'operations' without the use of instruments. With their bare hands they knead the abdomen of patients and appear to remove tissues that have the appearance of internal organs. However, when the 'extracted' tissues are analysed, they again prove to be of animal origin. These observations are instructive. Clearly, traditional healers are not above the use of bare-faced trickery; but not only do they get away with it, it also works. Charlatanism heals! How can this be?

Evidently the object extracted by the healer serves as a symbol of the disease. What matters is that the healer should possess the necessary power to make patients believe that their disease has been accurately diagnosed and cured. This is apparently what exorcists and hypnotists do, and it explains why so many traditional healers make use of trance. The patients' conviction that they are being cured is also, at its base, the 'placebo effect' that modern doctors do their best to eradicate, rather than put to therapeutic use.

Healing by exteriorization—the discharge of something inside that needs to be got out, as in the release of pus, the removal of foreign bodies or the exorcism of demons—is a healing procedure as old as time, as is the use of suggestion, the chief therapeutic instrument of healers right up to the present. The greatest modern exponent of these arcane practices, which he expertly disguised beneath an intricate web of scientific-sounding terminology, was Sigmund Freud.

The numerous accounts of Freud's life agree on his most salient qualities: his intellectual brilliance, his obsessive dedication to hard work, his outstanding gifts as a writer and extempore lecturer, his virtuoso ability to play with ideas and juggle them into new syntheses, his intolerance of criticism or dissent, his overriding ambition and his single-minded determination to succeed.

The 'indisputable favourite of his mother'

Freud was not unaware of the above characteristics in himself, though, naturally, he sometimes sought to play them down. He attributed his powerful ambition to several influences. First, there was the special love lavished on him by his young and beautiful mother, his elderly father Jacob's third wife. At the height of his fame, Freud wrote: 'A man who has been the indisputable favourite of his mother keeps for life the feeling of being a conqueror, that confidence of success which often induces real success' (*SE* [*Standard Edition*] 17, p. 156). Then there was a childhood event which occurred when he was seven or eight. For some reason he had urinated in his parents' bedroom. In an uncharacteristic flash of anger, his usually doting father cried, 'That boy will never amount to anything!' Recalling the incident, Freud commented, 'This must have been a terrible affront to my ambition, for allusions to this scene occur again and again in my dreams, and are constantly coupled with enumerations of my accomplishments and successes, as if I wanted to say: "You see, I have amounted to something after all." ' (Jones, Vol. 1, p. 93, Penguin edition).

Another memory that stayed with Freud, spurring him on to succeed, was an event recounted by his father: 'When I was a young fellow, one

Saturday,' Jacob Freud told him, 'I went for a walk in the streets of your birthplace, beautifully decked out, with a new fur cap on my head. Along comes a Christian, knocks off my cap into the muck with one blow, and shouts, "Jew, off the sidewalk!".' Shocked, Freud asked his father how he responded to this insult. His father meekly replied, 'I stepped into the road and picked up my cap.' The spectacle of his father grovelling in the gutter released fantasies of revenge in the young Sigmund and fuelled his determination to achieve celebrity in his chosen profession.

At school he proved a brilliant pupil, being first in his class seven years running, and his parents and teachers entertained high expectations of his future. In 1873 he enrolled at Vienna University to read medicine. Freud was particularly interested in zoology and neuroscience, and from 1876 to 1882 he combined his medical studies with research work at the Physiological Institute directed by Ernst Brücke (1819–1882). Brücke was the first of several exceptional men whom Freud was both to idolize and utilize as mentors to promote his career. Others were Theodor Meynert, Jean-Martin Charcot, Joseph Breuer and Wilhelm Fliess. A member of the generation that had rejected vitalism, Brücke was an outspoken determinist and materialist, whose declared objective was to reduce psychology to physiology, and physiology to physics and chemistry. Brücke's influence turned Freud into a lifelong determinist.

It was at Brücke's Institute that Freud met the eminent physician, Joseph Breuer (1842–1925), who stimulated his interest in hysteria. Freud's initial intention had been to follow a career in neurological research, but since there was no money in it and he lacked private means, he abandoned science and, having obtained his medical degree in 1881, decided to become a physician. He had fallen in love with his future wife, Martha Bernays, and became engaged to her in June 1882. He embarked on the required three years of hospital residency on a miserably low salary and, although his future prospects were bright, he knew it would be several years before he could expect to be able to support a wife and family—unless he could make an outstanding discovery that would bring him instant fame (Gay, 1988).

Hysteria and cocaine

From 1883 to 1886 Freud worked in the Psychiatric Department presided over by the illustrious Theodor Meynert (1833–1892). During this period, Freud experimented on himself and on others, including his fiancé, with cocaine, which at that time was thought of merely as a harmless and potentially useful alcaloid of coca. He found it to be an effective stimulant capable of countering the effects of fatigue, and published a paper proposing its use as a means of overcoming the disagreeable symptoms of withdrawal from morphine addiction. Fleishl, a friend of his, was addicted to morphine as a result of medical treatment for severe neuralgia. Freud took him into treatment. The result was predictable: Fleishl became addicted to cocaine in addition to morphine. Freud nevertheless published the case as a therapeutic success, even though he knew it to have been a miserable failure.

Ironically, Freud overlooked the one property of cocaine whose discovery would have brought him fame—its use as a local anaesthetic. He made a chance remark, however, to a colleague, Carl Koller, that cocaine caused numbness of the tongue. Acting on this hint, Koller tried it as an anaesthetic for operations on the eye with such dramatic success that he shot to the eminence that Freud was craving for himself. Freud, on the other hand, was excoriated by the medical establishment for not recognizing the danger that cocaine could lead to addiction.

Through the intervention of Brücke and Meynert, Freud obtained a travelling bursary which enabled him to spend the winter of 1885/86 in Paris, where he attended the lecture demonstrations on hysteria at the Salpétrière Hospital given by the famous neurologist Jean-Martin Charcot (1825–1893). Charcot believed that hysteria was a clinical entity with a clear psychopathology, and sought to prove the psychological origin of hysterical paralysis, fits and anaesthesia by inducing identical symptoms in healthy subjects and removing these symptoms through hypnotic suggestion. Freud at once fell under the great neurologist's spell, uncritically accepting his teaching. He seems to have adopted Charcot as a role model of the outstanding medical personality that he wished one day to become. Charcot was an autocrat, given to wild speculation, believing he could solve scientific problems through the force of his personality alone, and he would brook no dissent or criticism from pupils or colleagues.

The crucial idea that Freud brought back to Vienna from Charcot was that pathogenic ideas could lodge in an unconscious part of the mind where they were actually transformed into bodily symptoms. That mental events can have physical consequences was not a startling original insight: it is apparent, for example, in the sexual experience of us all—hence the joke that the penis must be the lightest object in the world since it can be raised by thought alone. What excited Freud was the idea that specifically unconscious ideas could give rise to pathology.

The origins of 'the talking cure'

Now fascinated by hysteria, he drew closer to Breuer. Together they collected material for a book, *Studies on Hysteria,* which was published in 1895. The first case presented in this book came to assume huge significance in the history of psychoanalysis. It concerned a young woman, aged 21 when she first consulted Breuer in 1880, whom for the sake of confidentiality they called 'Anna O.'.

Anna O. had become ill while nursing her father as he was dying of tuberculosis. Her illness began with a severe cough, followed by development of a rigid paralysis and loss of sensation in her right arm and leg, a convergent squint, and impaired vision and hearing. She had brief 'absences' of consciousness, when she would experience hallucinations and exhibit disturbed behaviour, shouting abuse at people and tearing buttons off her clothes. Her speech was disordered and she lost her capacity to speak German, her native tongue, and could converse only in English.

Breuer diagnosed the case as one of hysteria and he treated her until June 1882, when he discharged her from his care as being completely cured. The treatment he gave her became paradigmatic of the psychoanalytic approach. He visited her daily, usually in the evenings, when he encouraged her to recount what she had experienced during the course of the day. This 'unburdening process' had a calming effect and Anna seems to have become emotionally dependent on Breuer and on what she called her 'talking cure'.

One of her more bizarre symptoms was an inability to drink, despite a raging thirst. Under hypnosis, she recalled that this symptom had begun when she discovered her English companion's dog, which she disliked, drinking from a glass. She had said nothing about it at the time, but now she expressed anger, indignation and disgust at the incident. Following the recollection of this memory and the discharge ('abreaction') of the emotions involved, the symptom disappeared and she was able to drink without further difficulty.

This is said to have been a turning point both for Anna and for Breuer. In his published account of the case, he referred to the process of recall and abreaction as the 'therapeutic technical procedure', which, when systematically applied, should produce a successful outcome in all cases of hysteria. He took each of Anna's symptoms in chronological order of appearance, and encouraged her to remember the exact circumstances in which it had first occurred: as a result, he claimed, 'the symptom was permanently removed'.

The apparently successful technique used in the treatment of Anna O. provided Freud with the crucial ideas on which all his future theorizing would be based. It was, he believed, a revolutionary breakthrough in the psychological treatment of a severely debilitating illness. Yet there was little that was new or original about it. The notion that the physical symptoms of hysteria were due to some psychological or emotional trauma suffered in the past was borrowed directly from Charcot, and the idea that 'abreaction' brings 'catharsis' is very old indeed, belonging to the primordial aetiological theory of something bad that has to be got out of the system. Moreover, the 'confessional' aspect of the talking cure had been used by the Catholic Church to relieve guilt for centuries; and for the past twenty years the Viennese physician Moritz Benedikt had been teaching that hysteria was caused by a 'pathogenic secret' rooted in the sex life of the patient (Ellenberger, 1970).

What was new in Breuer and Freud's contribution was the idea that the memory of the trauma responsible for hysterical symptoms was suppressed: for it was the suppressed or 'strangulated' affects caused by the trauma which, they believed, were converted into physical symptoms. The 'therapeutic technical procedure' worked, they maintained, because it offered an alternative mode of release for the affect: it could be discharged in words rather than turned into symptoms.

This was the seminal idea from which psychoanalysis grew and it was to prove a major influence on psychiatric thinking in the twentieth century, especially in the treatment of war neuroses, such as 'shell shock' and post-traumatic stress disorder.

According to Breuer, Anna's treatment ended when she reported a terrifying hallucination of a snake, 'which constituted the root of her whole illness' and she at once recovered her ability to speak German. She left Vienna and we are told that, after a while, regained her mental balance entirely. 'Since then,' concluded Breuer, 'she had enjoyed complete health.' It was apparently a miraculous cure of a young woman who had suffered a crippling illness; and its publication brought considerable prestige to Freud as well as Breuer. For many years, it was regarded as the classic example of a successful cathartic cure and its achievement did much to support Freud's later claims for the therapeutic effectiveness of psychoanalysis.

However, we now know that the true facts of the case were very different. Anna O.'s real name was Bertha Pappenheim. In later years she was to become a pioneer social worker, taking a leading role in the struggle for women's rights and in providing relief for refugees and orphans. Through brilliant detective work, the psychiatric historian Henri Ellenberger discovered that she was admitted to Kreuzlingen Sanatorium on Lake Constance in July 1882, only a month after Breuer had discharged her as cured. Her medical records, which are still extant, reveal, as Ellenberger caustically observed, that 'the famed "prototype of a cathartic cure" was neither a cure nor a catharsis' (Ellenberger, 1993). On admission to Kreuzlingen the 'completely cured' Bertha Pappenheim was still complaining of hallucinations, convulsions, recurring loss of the ability to speak German and severe facial neuralgia. As if this were not bad enough, she had also become addicted to morphine, which Breuer had prescribed for her neuralgia.

As Ellenberger's shocking discoveries demonstrate, Breuer's and Freud's claims to have cured Bertha Pappenheim were fraudulent—as fraudulent as Freud's earlier claim to have cured Fleishl's morphine addiction by giving him cocaine. Moreover, many have argued that Bertha Pappenheim was not suffering from hysteria at all, and have offered alternative diagnoses, such as a left-sided cerebral lesion (which might account for her speech disorder and right-sided paralysis and loss of sensation), tubercular meningitis, syphilis, a borderline personality disorder, or even that the entire illness was simulated. It has subsequently emerged that Bertha Pappenheim herself guided and to a large extent controlled her own treatment, and a plausible interpretation of Breuer's actual case notes (as opposed to his published account) is that, once she had been introduced to the cathartic method, she used it to hold and manipulate Breuer's attention.

Whether there was an underlying physical illness or not, Breuer certainly did not cure her, and Freud knew it. Not only did she spend three and a half months in Kreuzlingen in 1882, but between 1883 and 1887 she was admitted on three subsequent occasions to the Inzersdorf Sanatorium, altogether for a total of ten months' in-patient treatment. On each admission the diagnosis was 'hysteria'. Freud was intimately aware of these facts, for on two occasions in 1887, Martha Bernays, whom he had married the previous year, wrote to her mother specifically mentioning Anna O. and reporting that, although she was normal during the daytime, her hallucinations returned in the evening. Fortunately, by the end of the 1880s, Bertha Pappenheim was free of symptoms and it seems that they never returned, leaving her free to live a socially productive life. But it was little thanks to Breuer or to Freud.

Freud's knowledge of the ineffectiveness of Breuer's treatment of this case did not discourage him from basing his future theoretical formulations on it. The urgency with which he felt himself driven to achieve professional celebrity encouraged him to seize on each new idea as it occurred to him as a 'discovery' of historic significance. Fame was the spur. There was no time to be wasted on the diligent collection of evidence to support (or refute) what he had 'discovered'. The 1890s were for Freud a period of theoretical exuberance.

Psychoanalysis is born: the basic concepts

With a disregard for correct scientific procedure that was to prove characteristic of him, and giving free wing to an imagination fuelled with regular doses of cocaine, Freud proceeded to outline the basic concepts of what, in 1896, he first referred to as 'psychoanalysis'. These concepts—*repression, resistance, conflict, transference,* and the use of *free association* and *dream analysis* as a means of advancing the 'talking cure'—were all elaborations of the fundamental principle of catharsis, which was erroneously alleged to have been so successful in the treatment of Bertha Pappenheim.

Like Breuer, Freud at first used hypnosis, not to implant positive suggestions for health but to assist patients to recall the origins of their symptoms, for 'hysterics', maintained Breuer and Freud, 'suffer mainly from reminiscences'. The reminiscences concerned were often shameful or disagreeable and consequently people were understandably reluctant to recall or reproduce them. This reluctance Freud called 'resistance'. The mechanism responsible for making the reminiscence unconscious (active forgetting), he called 'repression', and the concept of repression became the cornerstone of psychoanalytic theory. Repression was responsible for 'intrapsychic conflict'—the struggle between the emotion that sought its own discharge in consciousness and the forces of repression that kept it unconscious. The repressed affect, denied all other forms of expression, discharged itself in the production of neurotic symptoms. Treatment required the use of techniques to release what was repressed. The symptoms should then disappear. This again was the primordial story of something pathological inside a patient that had to be let out, like pus inside an abscess requiring surgical release.

Finding the induction of hypnosis an unreliable method, Freud sought other techniques for rendering the emotionally charged reminiscences conscious. In the course of treating 'Elizabeth von R.', the first full-length analysis of hysteria that he undertook, he hit on the use of 'free association' that was to provide the 'basic rule' of psychoanalysis. Lying relaxed on a couch, patients were instructed to report whatever came into their minds, rather like a passenger in a railway train reporting on the scene as it passes before the window. *Everything* had to be reported, however trivial, embarrassing or offensive it might be.

In the case of Elizabeth von R., the crux was reached when, according to Freud, he offered her the interpretation (which she strenuously resisted) that she was in love with her brother-in-law and that she had repressed wicked desires for her sister's death. Freud reported that when he was able to overcome her resistance and she eventually accepted his interpretation, her symptoms disappeared. This again seems to have been untrue. Elizabeth von R.'s real name was Ilona Weiss and, many years later, she told her daughter that contrary to Freud's claims she had not been helped by seeing him. '[He tried] to persuade me that I was in love with my brother-in-law', she said, 'but that wasn't so.' (Webster, 1997).

Charcot had given Freud the idea that hysterical symptoms were caused by sexual traumata in the past: 'C'est toujours la chose sexuelle. Toujours! Toujours!' he declared in his excited, emphatic manner. Freud was evidently determined to capitalize on this idea and use it as the basis for his own theory of neurosis. The trouble was that many patients would not oblige him by producing sexual memories to order. To solve this problem he took one of the theoretical leaps so characteristic of him. The failure of patients to confirm his theory would not be allowed to persuade him that the theory was wrong. Rather the patient must be held responsible for covering up and concealing the truth. Failing to produce the required sexual memory was entirely due to resistance. Building on this idea Freud went on to assert that resistance to reproducing the memory was the same force that had driven the memory out of consciousness in the first place. Thus resistance and repression were two aspects of the same dynamic principle responsible for keeping unpleasant sexual memories unconscious and for keeping the patient ill; and successful treatment must depend on overcoming the resistance, undoing the repression and making the traumatic memory conscious.

Developing these hunches into the basic theoretical framework for the practice of psychoanalysis, Freud displayed the sleight of hand of an accomplished magician, who, having covertly slipped a rabbit into his hat, proceeds to produce it to the gratifying applause of his audience. Generations of psychoanalysts continued to applaud this imposture, believing that Freud's 'discovery' of the sexual cause of the neuroses was derived from his acute clinical observation of a large number of cases. In fact, it was a conjecture formed while treating a small number of cases, whose clinical details were constantly recycled in the psychoanalytic literature.

There can be little doubt that while patients were undergoing treatment at the hands of Breuer or Freud some of their symptoms would have disappeared. This could certainly have been due to the rapport that they established with their patients, but it could equally have been because neurotic symptoms tend spontaneously to come and go over a period of time. Freud was reluctantly forced to acknowledge, as he treated more and more patients by his method, that symptoms had an unfortunate habit of returning. This put him in something of a quandary: how was he to explain it? It must be, he decided, because there were earlier and certainly nastier sexual experiences that the patient was refusing to re-member. Inevitably, these must be sexual and probably, Freud assumed, due to a premature and precocious introduction of the patient as a child to a form of sexual involvement that she was incapable of accepting and therefore experienced as traumatic.

Sexual seduction: fact or fiction?

With this hunch Freud's theory of sexual seduction was born. It was a piece of theoretical guesswork, which, resurrected by Jeffrey Masson, was to bring misery to thousands of families through the 'recovered memory syndrome' and its attendant industry run by therapists who claimed to be able to diagnose and treat the trauma which they insisted had been inflicted on their patients, even though the patients had no recollection of the alleged abuse.

Jeffrey Masson's *The Assault on Truth* (1984, revised 1992) was well named, for his book is as much a travesty of clinical reality as anything perpetuated by Freud. Masson puts into emotive language the hitherto widely accepted belief that Freud's theory of sexual seduction was based upon factual memories recalled by his patients in analysis:

> Freud's female patients had the courage to face what had happened to them in childhood—often this included violent scenes of rape by a fa-ther—and to communicate their traumas to Freud, no doubt hesitating to believe their own memories and reluctant to remember the deep shame and hurt they had felt. Freud listened and understood and gave them permis-sion to remember these terrible events.

It is now clear, however, that far from giving them permission to re-member and speak of these terrible events, Freud himself attributed the seduction to his patients, believing that such experiences would provide the 'sexual trauma' that he wished to establish as the indispensable aetio-logical factor in hysteria. He himself described analytic treatment as a procedure designed to coerce patients to recollect sexually traumatic scenes of which they had no recollection. His whole theory of hysteria rested on the doctrine that sexual seduction in childhood would have pathological consequences *only if the patient had no conscious memory of the event*. The patient then had to be forced into acknowledging that she had indeed experienced such a trauma. Her resistance to having such disagreeable incidents attributed to her was often so stubborn that to overcome it demanded in Freud's own words 'the strongest compulsion of the treatment'. Masson's argument that Freud knew that his patients had been seduced and that he later abandoned the seduction theory out of professional cowardice can thus be rejected.

Freud proceeded to divide the neuroses into two groups: the *actual neuroses*, whose source he considered to reside in the present sex life of the patient, and the *psychoneuroses*, whose source lay in the patient's past sex life. He subdivided the actual neuroses into 'neurasthenia' (whose origin he thought was masturbation) and 'anxiety neurosis' (caused by coitus interruptus), and the psychoneuroses into 'hysteria' and 'obsessional neurosis' (both the result of sexual abuse suffered in childhood). Hysteria occurred mainly in females, who suffered the abuse passively; obsessional neurosis occurred mainly in males, who participated more actively in the abusive experience and felt pleasure (their obsessive ideas being a form of self-reproach for having experienced illicit enjoyment). Freud claimed that he had analysed eighteen cases of hysteria and 'discovered' that in every case the patient had been seduced in childhood. This, he alleged, was a discovery of such enormous importance that he felt justified in comparing it to 'the source of the Nile in neuropathology'. Within a year, however, he was admitting to his friend Wilhelm Fliess that he no longer believed in the truth of this 'discovery'.

The sexual seduction theory provided him with a pat explanation for the aetiology of neurotic conditions, but there were problems with it which made Freud uneasy. To begin with, psychoneurosis is very common. Was he to assume that Viennese children were being routinely abused by their adult caretakers on a pandemic scale? As Freud acknowledged, both he and his brothers and sisters had neurotic symptoms. Did this mean that his kindly old father had sexually interfered with them all in their early years? Moreover, for an impecunious practitioner to embrace such a theory would scarcely encourage the growth of a thriving practice if the fathers who paid him fees to analyse their neurotic daughters received little more for their pains than the accusation of being monsters of sexual depravity. On due reflection, Freud decided that he had better retreat: accordingly, he wrote to Fliess in 1897 to say that he 'no longer believed in [his] *neurotica*' (theory of neurosis).

Forced to abandon the seduction theory, what could he put in its place? Should he renounce the sexual aetiology of the neuroses altogether? Decidedly not, for that would be to defenestrate the baby with the bath water and to reject the teaching of the great Charcot. A solution occurred to him. What if his patients had not been actually seduced in childhood but had produced *fantasies* of being seduced? What if, as young children, they had wished to be seduced only to become ashamed of such wishful fantasies and, as a consequence, later repress them? That would provide a satisfactory resolution of the problem. Fathers of his patients would be spared scandalous recrimination, for no one could be held responsible for erotic fantasies concocted by a child. Moreover, if the patients in Freud's care failed to report such fantasies then the remedy was easy: they would be told that it was because they had repressed them. If further free associations on the couch failed to overcome the repression, and the memory of such fantasies stubbornly failed to re-emerge, then patients would be told it was because they were resisting treatment. As a result, Freud replaced the seduction theory with the more sustainable but no less controversial theory of *infantile sexuality*.

The sexual theory: 'an unshakeable bulwark'

That Freud could be ruthless in overcoming resistance and insistent that patients should produce the repressed sexual traumas he wanted to hear about is apparent from his writings. 'Before they come for analysis', Freud wrote in his paper "The Aetiology of Hysteria", 'the patients know nothing about these scenes. They are indignant as a rule if we warn them that such scenes are going to emerge. Only the strongest compulsion of the treatment can induce them to embark on a reproduction of them' (*SE* 3, p. 304). When patients on the couch fell silent, this too was to be taken as resistance, and dealt with accordingly. When patients protested that nothing occurred to them to say, that was absolutely not acceptable. 'We must not believe what they say,' Freud wrote in another paper, 'we must always assume, and tell them too, that they have kept something back . . . We must insist on this, we must repeat the pressure and represent ourselves as infallible, till at last we are really told something' (*SE* 2, p. 279).

The blatant use of such unscrupulous tactics may have enabled him to bully his patients into accepting his interpretations, but clinical arrogance of this degree of magnitude was ill-designed to protect him against the kind of missed physical diagnosis of which all psychotherapists live in dread. Almost inevitably, this fate befell Freud. For example, a little girl was sent to him suffering abdominal pains. He diagnosed her as an 'unmistakable' case of hysteria and 'cured' her with psychoanalysis. Two months after he discharged her she died, the cause being an abdominal lymphoma. Apparently unabashed, Freud denied all culpability, insisting that he had cured the hysteria which, he declared, 'had used the tumour as a provoking cause'.

Freud's famous theory of sexuality, which he developed in the years 1897 to 1905, was based on the notion of an instinctual drive which existed a priori in the individual as a biological given and passed through three stages in the course of ontogeny (personal development). Here Freud felt he had his feet on solid ground. Not only is sex indispensable to the survival of the species but, under Darwin's influence, Freud understood sexual selection to be a primary factor in evolution. His sexual theory could thus provide psychoanalysis with a sound organic basis in biology and would enable him to create the science of psychobiology that he had set himself to achieve. Sex provided him with the essential link, connecting the body to the mind, and would enable him to fulfil Brücke's prediction that the neuroses would prove to have a physical cause. Inspired with this vision he wrote his 'Project for a Scientific Psychology'. 'In the sexual process', he was to write to Jung in April 1908, 'we have the indispensable organic foundation without which a medical man can only feel ill at ease in the life of the psyche' (*Freud/Jung Letters*, pp. 140–41).

In reducing the sum total of human motivations to sex Freud was adopting an incredibly narrow perspective, but this could not have been so apparent to him as it is to us. Ethology, the branch of biological science that studies animal behaviour in natural habitats, had yet to be born, and Freud knew nothing of the rich diversity of instinctual patterns occurring in nature, for the zoology of his time confined its observations to animals in zoos, where opportunities for actualizing the vast repertoire of instinctive potential inherent in all animal species were lacking. When territorial and dominance conflicts are ruled out by lack of space and an absence of competitors, it is little wonder that bored, well-nourished animals pass their days in fornication or 'self-abuse'. That Freud's patients displayed a reluctance to become loquacious when asked about their sexual history and showed signs of embarrassment when the issue was raised is understandable in view of the sexual inhibitions current in the society of his time. That we are less inhibited in this respect is perhaps a measure of the effect that Freud's ideas have had on our culture.

In this manner Freud's association with Charcot and Breuer gave him the inspiration to use sex as the means to graft psychological ideas on to the physiological principles he had acquired from Brücke and, to his own satisfaction, ground the theory and techniques of psychoanalysis in biology. Sex became the bedrock on which Freud's entire edifice was raised. 'My dear Jung', he said on one much quoted occasion, 'promise me never to abandon the sexual theory. That is the most essential thing of all. You see, we must make a dogma of it, an unshakeable bulwark' (Jung, *MDR*, p. 173). Neurotic symptoms, the symbolism of dreams, perversions, jokes, slips of the tongue, the psychopathology of everyday life, all were made to rest on this single 'indispensable foundation', sex.

Why Freud insisted on this rigid and excessive reductionism was probably out of a misguided belief that he was being scientific and obeying Occam's razor (namely, that in scientific explanations entities should not be multiplied beyond necessity). Like all nineteenth-century physicians Freud was much impressed by the germ theory of disease proposed by Koch and Pasteur, to the effect that all genuine diseases have but a single cause. Charcot had taught him that hysteria was a genuine disease. Freud likewise assumed that other neuroses, such as obsessional neurosis and 'neurasthenia' were also genuine diseases and persuaded himself that he had discovered the single cause responsible for them all. On this discovery he was to rest his hopes of fame. With it he could fulfil his lifelong ambition of 'opening all secrets with a single key'. Henceforth, colleagues or patients who questioned or refused to accept this claim were treated as heretics and cast into outer darkness, as Jung, Adler, Stekel, Rank, Ferenczi and others were to discover.

Right up to the middle years of his life, Freud was prone to hero-worship men whom he perceived as intellectual giants. In addition to Brücke, Meynert, Charcot and Breuer, he was later to be in thrall to the brilliant and intensely charismatic Swiss psychiatrist Carl Gustav Jung (1875–1961).

From the standpoint of the development of psychoanalysis, the most influential and certainly the most eccentric of these hero figures was the Berlin ENT surgeon Wilhelm Fliess with whom Freud corresponded through much of the 1890s. This correspondence provides major insights into the course of Freud's thinking, and it also reveals the extent of his credulity.

Fliess believed in the essential bisexuality of human beings and maintained that the whole life span of both sexes was determined by different rhythmic cycles, the female cycle being 28 days and male cycle 23 days. These cycles, according to Fliess, controlled the dates of birth, illnesses and death, as well as the regenerative processes on which life depends. He also believed there to be an essential psychophysical correspondence between the genitals and the nasal mucosa, and described a syndrome which he called the 'nasal reflex neurosis', which could be relieved by a most unpleasant operation on the nasal septum.

All these ideas Freud enthusiastically embraced as the revolutionary discoveries of a scientific genius. As their epistolary relationship progressed, Freud's admiration for Fliess grew, to the extent that he could address him, without embarrassment, as 'the Kepler of Biology' and his 'Messiah'. However, apart from the menstrual cycle, no evidence has ever been forthcoming in support of Fliess's rhythms or his nasal reflex neurosis and they have gone the way of all unsubstantiated conjectures.

Freud's 'creative illness': self-analysis and the function of dreams

During the period 1894 to 1899 Freud suffered what Henri Ellenberger (1970) has called a 'creative illness' and his emotional dependence on Fliess intensified. In his letters Freud complained of feeling isolated in a hostile world, of being unable to shake off worrying psychosomatic symptoms, and of suffering mood swings that alternated alarmingly between elation and despair. His psychosomatic complaints included cardiac arrhythmias, shortness of breath, fear of dying, headaches and recurrent sinusitis. The mood swings and sinusitis could be accounted for by Freud's psychological dependency on cocaine, while his irregular heartbeat and breathing difficulties are attributable to his addiction to cigars, which he considered a substitute for masturbation. But as Ellen-berger points out, it was during this period of 'creative illness' that most of Freud's major insights and theoretical formulations occurred. These were probably inspired, and certainly energized, by cocaine.

The crowning achievement of these years, Freud always maintained, was his 'discovery' of the function of dreams and how to interpret them. Wishing to understand the cause of his symptoms, which he attributed to psychological rather than physical origins, Freud embarked on a pro-tracted course of self-analysis, which included keeping a careful record of his dreams and using free association to elucidate their meaning. In the early morning of July 24th, 1895, he had a dream that has gone down in history as 'the dream of Irma's injection'. He was staying with his family at Schloss Belle Vue, a favourite resort on the outskirts of Vienna. As he worked on the dream later that day, the thought suddenly struck him that *it was the fulfilment of a hidden wish*. This flash of illumination brought with it the conviction that he had found the key to unlock the door to the unconscious mind. At that precise moment he knew that the riddle of dreams, which had preoccupied oneirologists for millennia, had been solved, and he entertained the fantasy that one day a marble tablet would be affixed to the facade of the schloss stating that 'In this house on July 24th, 1895, the Secret of Dreams was Revealed to Dr Sigm. Freud'—a fantasy that was subsequently implemented in reality.

The Interpretation of Dreams, completed in 1899, was to dominate theoretical approaches to dreaming for much of the twentieth century. Freud offers the dream of Irma's injection as the prototypical example of Freudian dream analysis, and there is a rich irony in this, for the dream is about one of Freud's patients who approaches him at a party with the disagreeable information that, despite his treatment, her illness has not improved but got worse. In the dream he deals with this news in a way that we can now see as typical of him: he blames the patient, accusing her of resisting his interpretation of her case. Then he proceeds to pass the blame on to a medical colleague. The crucial wish motivating the dream, as Freud honestly acknowledged, was the desire not to be the one held responsible for Irma's deterioration. Although there is evident sex symbolism in the dream (for example, the colleague responsible for her relapse has given her an injection with a dirty syringe), Freud glosses over this, stressing that the primary wish is to escape blame. This is odd in view of the emphasis on sexual motivation that dominates the rest of his book.

Freud's theory of dreams is an extension of his theory of neurosis. The wish of which the dream is a fulfilment is a repressed wish—repressed because it is unacceptable (usually sexual) and, if permitted to reach dream consciousness, would shock the sleeper into wakefulness. Because of the vigilance of a psychic institution that Freud termed the *censor*, the repressed wish (the *latent* content of the dream) can only be expressed in disguised form (the *manifest* content). The dream thus circumvents inner tensions that would otherwise wake the dreamer, for dreaming permits the vicarious fulfilment of the forbidden wish. Thus, in Freud's famous formulation, 'dreams are the guardians of sleep'. The purpose of dream analysis is to make the latent content of the dream conscious. Since the use of free association makes this possible, Freud regarded dreams as providing 'the royal road to the unconscious', and, as a result, the analysis of dreams became an essential part of classical psychoanalytic technique.

That dreams might reflect sexual wishes was not a new idea: it had already been noted by such authorities as Charcot, Janet and Krafft-Ebing. What was ingenious about Freud's approach to dreaming was the use to which he put this idea. Had he maintained that all dreams were overt fulfilments of wishes, his theory could readily have been refuted but he was careful not to do this. What he claimed was that dreams were disguised wish fulfilments and this again put his theory beyond refutation. If, for example, a patient dreamed of something happening that clearly she would not have wished to happen to her, then Freud interpreted the dream as a wish on the part of the dreamer to prove his theory wrong! To engage Freud in an argument was always to be on the losing side. Like the builder of the *Titanic*, Freud designed his brainchild to be unsinkable.

The unconscious as a repository of repressed wishes

Similar ingenuity is apparent in Freud's whole concept of the unconscious. He could not claim to have discovered the unconscious, for the idea was already current by the time he entered the scene. What was novel about Freud's approach was his idea that the unconscious was the part of the mind whose specific function it was to harbour repressed impulses, memories and thoughts. It was useless for his critics to object that they harboured no such impulses or memories in themselves, because Freud would counter that they could not know them precisely because they were unconscious and they preferred to keep them that way. Only psychoanalysis possessed the ability to make them conscious. Thus, his critics were trapped in an ingenious catch-22.

Much of the background to the dream of Irma's injection is revealed in the correspondence between Freud and Fleiss (Masson, 1985). It emerges that Irma was a composite figure, created by Freud's unconscious, based on two young widows who were patients of his. One of these was Emma Eckstein, who suffered from constant pain and bleeding from her nose. Freud's interpretation of these symptoms was that they were psychosomatic manifestations of repressed sexual desire for her analyst—that she was, in fact, 'bleeding for love' of him. Her symptoms persisted, however, and suspecting this was a case of 'nasal reflex neurosis', he called in Fliess, who operated on her, removing her nasal septum. Not only was this traumatic operation entirely unnecessary, but Fliess botched it, carelessly leaving behind a gauze pack in one nasal cavity, which turned septic. When this was found and removed two weeks later by another surgeon, Emma Eckstein had a severe haemorrhage, which in less expert hands may well have proved fatal. This was an evident piece of malpractice that Freud was careful to conceal in his published associations to the dream. But the dream itself is evidence of his continuing unease about the case, and his desire to be absolved of guilt and responsibility for his role in it.

In the light of modern dream research, it is now clear that most of Freud's ideas about dreams were wrong. For him, dreams were produced in the same way as neurotic symptoms, and this implied that normal, well-adjusted people would not have them. Dream laboratory studies have established, however, that dreaming sleep is an entirely normal and recurrent state of sleep in all mammals, including ourselves. We spend about a quarter of every night in REM (rapid eye-movement) dreaming sleep. According to Freud, the basic need of mental life was to achieve a state of tranquility through the complete discharge of all tensions. He later called this the Nirvana principle. For him, the healthy person, untroubled by dreams, was a bonded heterosexual with a regular and satisfying sex life, who could discharge his or her sexual tensions in repeated orgasms and enjoy a recurrent state of tensionless Nirvana. There is little objective evidence to support this view, and much to refute it.

Freud's assumptions about the ways in which the central nervous system functions were deeply flawed, based as they were on the neurobiology of the 1880s. He believed it to be an essentially passive organization, responsive only to outer stimulation, and incapable of generating either its own energy or its own information. The Freudian view of the psyche and nervous system, as fuelled by powerful drives (sex and later aggression) like a train driven by coal and steam, is hopelessly obsolete and quaint. No one now conceives of human or animal psychology in the engineering terms that still seemed appropriate at the end of the nineteenth century. Although later developments in Freudian 'ego psychology' contributed some advance on Freud's original thinking, its contribution is of dubious significance because it still clung to Freud's mechanistic model. Thanks to the research of the last sixty years, we now know that the nervous system is metabolically capable of generating (and cancelling) its own energy and genetically capable of producing much of its own information. We also know that episodes of REM sleep and dreaming occur as a result of the spontaneous activity of the central nervous system, acting independently of stimuli arising from the environment.

It seems likely that Freud realized that the neurobiology he had learned from Brücke could become outdated, for he eventually disowned any relationship between neuroscience and psychoanalysis, and suppressed his 'Project for a Scientific Psychology'. He wanted his theories to appear original and to survive any revolutionary or unforeseen developments that might occur in neuroscientific research. Nevertheless, his notion of repressed sexual 'libido' which could discharge itself in the manifest content of dreams, the symptoms of neurotic illness, perverse sexual acts and inadvertent slips of the tongue, was the product of the now wholly discredited teaching he received in Brücke's laboratory.

But such was the brilliance of Freud's rhetoric, his diligence and powers of political manipulation that his franchise on psychodynamic thinking has persisted to the detriment of psychotherapeutic practice as a whole. Because psychoanalysis has clung onto the outdated a priori assumptions of its founder, it has resisted scientific verification (or refutation) and languished in an intellectual time warp of its own making. There are signs, however, that this is beginning to change, with the emergence of a new evolutionary paradigm that could drag psychoanalysis out of its sterile state of self-absorbed isolation. We shall return to this possibility later on.

Infantile sexuality

Having abandoned the seduction theory, Freud persisted in his view that neurosis was associated with disturbances of sexual function in the earliest years of childhood, as a result of which the child's sexual development became partially arrested or 'fixated' at an immature stage. To his contemporaries the idea that the 'component instincts' of sexuality became apparent in the 'polymorphously perverse' behaviour and fantasies of infancy, as Freud now maintained, was only marginally less shocking than the idea that neurosis was due to early sexual abuse. But it was a sustainable hypothesis supported by observation, since young children do display such precursors of adult sexual behaviour as penile erections, 'clasping' and pelvic thrust. Where Freud allowed his theoretical enthusiasm to carry him beyond the pale of biological probability was in proposing that development of the sexual instinct proceeds through a series of stages involving the mouth and the anus before reaching the final genital stage, which a child was assumed to reach by the age of about five.

Observation could certainly confirm that young children derive pleasure from the acts of sucking, feeding, urinating and defecation; but where Freud put himself on impossibly shaky ground was his uncritical acceptance of Wilhelm Fliess's view that this pleasure was exclusively sexual in nature. This would presume that sex is the only form of pleasure available to us, which is evidently not the case. For good evolutionary reasons, nature has arranged things so that many activities that promote individual survival give rise to pleasure, just as activities or stimuli which threaten survival give rise to fear or pain. Eating, drinking and playing (by which young animals practise behaviours essential for self-preservation) are all pleasurable in their own right and it is clear that sex is but one of many delights that children and adults can enjoy. It is true that use of the mouth and anus as 'erogenous zones' can be involved in the arousal associated with sexual foreplay in adults, but this in no way proves that the pleasure derived from oral or anal stimulation in childhood is intrinsically sexual.

Yet Freud developed an elaborate theoretical system around this idea, maintaining that a variety of 'perversions' and neuroses, as well as 'oral' and 'anal' character structures, were due to fixations of (sexual) libido in these earlier stages of development and to defences against the unacceptable desires arising from them. In a mischievous lampoon of the sexual theory, Richard Webster (1997) has suggested that the feet and hands should be added to Freud's list of 'erogenous zones' to provide 'pedal' and 'manual' stages of libidinal development. A child's delight in having its feet tickled and its evident desire to hold onto its mother's hand would then be diagnosed as manifestations of 'pedal-eroticism' and 'manual-eroticism' respectively; and soccer and handball could be interpreted as polymorphously perverse activities!

As one might expect, Freud's one-track mind determined his understanding of dream symbolism as much as his elucidation of symptom formation. Just as a dream sword being thrust into its scabbard had to be symbolic of intercourse, so an hysterical loss of consciousness symbolized orgasm; appendicitis or vomiting represented pregnancy wishes; dyspnoea (shortness of breath) symbolized coital breathing; a nervous cough represented fellatio; and squeezing blackheads, the act of masturbation. 'It is fair to say', declared Freud, 'that there is no group of ideas that is incapable of representing sexual facts and wishes.' He felt justified in reducing a vast array of objects to their supposed male or female sexual symbolism:

All elongated objects, such as sticks, tree-trunks and umbrellas (the opening of these last being comparable to an erection) may stand for the male organ —as well as all long, sharp weapons, such as knives, daggers and pikes. Another frequent though not entirely intelligible symbol of the same thing is a nail file—possibly on account of the rubbing up and down. Boxes, cases, chests, cupboards and ovens represent the uterus, and also hollow objects, ships, and vessels of all kinds. Rooms in dreams are usually women; if the various ways in and out of them are represented, this interpretation is scarcely open to doubt … A dream of going through a suite of rooms is a brothel or harem dream … Steps, ladders or staircases, or, as the case may be, walking up or down them, are representations of the sexual act.

In men's dreams a necktie often appears as a symbol for the penis ... nor is there any doubt that all weapons and tools are used as symbols for the male organ: e.g., ploughs, hammers, rifles, revolvers, daggers, sabres, etc. (Freud, 1976, pp. 470–73).

The banal reductiveness of such interpretations robs these symbols of all their other implications. While all these objects may indeed represent the human genitals and sexual activities, they may also represent a lot of other things as well. As Jung once quipped, the penis is itself a phallic symbol. Nature clearly intended it to represent power and virility as well as male sexuality (this could explain why the human penis is proportionately three times larger than in any other primate; Diamond, 1991).

The fundamentally reductive approach which characterized the Freudian attitude to the phenomena of life—what Jung was to caricature as the 'nothing but' approach, which boiled all things down to their lowest common denominator—helped to spread what many have seen as the disenchantment and spiritual impoverishment endemic in our culture. The more perceptive of Freud's disciples recognized their complicity in this misfortune: 'We must grudgingly admit', wrote Erik Erikson (1962), 'that even as we were trying to devise, with scientific determinism, a therapy for the few, we were led to promote an ethical disease among the many.'

Oedipus castrated

A highly significant 'unacceptable desire' was thought to occur at the phallic stage when, Freud maintained, a boy becomes sexually interested in his mother, wishes to possess her and to displace his father in her affections. However, this 'Oedipal situation' gives rise to fears that his father will retaliate and punish him by castration. The resulting 'castration complex' is reinforced by the boy's discovery that girls lack a penis and by the thought that this deficiency could be the result of castration.

On what evidence did Freud base this apparently far-fetched scenario? The Fliess correspondence once more gives us the lead. On 15 October 1897, Freud wrote: 'A single idea of general value dawned on me. I have found, in my own case too, [the phenomenon of] being in love with my mother and jealous of my father, and I now consider it a universal event in early childhood.'

As with his other major 'discoveries', Freud managed to present this 'universal event in early childhood' in such a way as to make it seem a phenomenon which he had detected in the course of studying large numbers of cases. In fact, it was based on two speculations: (1) that he may have been sexually aroused when he saw his mother undressing (if he had seen her undressing, he was not sure) when he travelled with her from Leipzig to Vienna in a railway sleeping compartment as a young child of three years-old, and (2) that the erections which Fliess reported observing in his one-year-old son, Robert, may have been caused by seeing his mother in the nude. From these intuitive guesses, Freud generalized a family drama to the whole of humanity and formally dedicated the Oedipus complex as the keystone of the arch of psychoanalytic theory.

Despite its insubstantial origins, the Oedipus complex and its resolution by the castration complex became psychoanalytic dogmas accepted without question by generations of Freud's followers. One of the very few to express dissent was the 'independent' British psychoanalyst John Bowlby, who argued that while it was undeniable that children become strongly attached to their mothers, this has little if anything to do with sex and everything to do with the ubiquitous, naturally occurring mother–child bond apparent in a great number of animal species. Sons may indeed perceive fathers as rivals for their mother's love, but on the whole fathers do not subject their offspring to threats of castration in order to eliminate the competition for their wives' affections.

In an important reassessment of Freud's case histories, Frank Sulloway (1991) reveals the extent to which they are all characterized by arbitrary interpretations and ineffective outcome. Indeed, Frederick Crews has questioned whether Freud himself ever practised psychoanalysis in the manner which he recommended to others. Rather than allowing patients' free associations to lead naturally to repressed material, 'he sought to "nail" the client with hastily conceived interpretations which he then drove home unabatingly'.

Disturbing case histories

Perhaps the most upsetting of Freud's case histories, particularly to feminists, is that of 'Dora' (Ida Bauer), published by Freud in 1905 as a 'Fragment of an Analysis of a Case of Hysteria'. This was regarded by generations of psychoanalysts as 'the classical analysis of the structure and genesis of hysteria' (Erik Erikson, 1962).

Ida Bauer was an attractive young woman of 18 when she was brought reluctantly to see Freud. She suffered from numerous tics, suicidal thoughts, and had become extremely impertinent to her parents. The dramatis personae involved in the story she unfolds are her parents and their friends Herr and Frau K. Herr Bauer, Ida's father, was having an affair with Frau K., while Herr K. had shown sexual interest in Ida since she was fourteen, when he had forced a kiss on her, which she found disgusting. Herr K. followed this up by offering Ida a direct sexual invitation two years later, for which she slapped his face. She told her mother about these incidents, insisting that her father should break off relations with the K.s. When Herr Bauer tackled him, however, Herr K. denied the incident had ever occurred and attributed Ida's story to a fevered imagination stimulated by romantic literature. To Ida's fury Herr Bauer accepted Herr K.'s assurances and refused to give way to her pressure to stop seeing the K.s. Ida retaliated by accusing her father of colluding with Herr K. in his designs so that he could continue his affair with Frau K. Deeply embarrassed by this 'insubordinate' line of reasoning, Herr Bauer brought his troublesome daughter to Dr Freud.

What is shocking about Freud's approach to this case is that he did not take his patient's part in this steamy drama, but rather that of her father and Herr K. Freud told Ida that she was really in love with Herr K. and that her disgust when he kissed her was an hysterical reaction to feeling his erect penis pressing against her (this was entirely Freud's supposition of which Ida denied all knowledge). Freud went on to suggest that when Ida slapped Herr K.'s face, it 'was by no means a final No'.

Not for a moment does Freud entertain the possibility that a 14-year-old girl might appropriately be disgusted by the advances of a much older man. Rather he attributes her behaviour to psychosexual pathology based on the usual Freudian credo of repressed homosexuality, fantasies of pregnancy and oral sex, memories of childhood masturbation, and an early witnessing of the 'primal scene' of her parents having sexual intercourse. But Ida would have none of this, and, totally rejecting Freud's interpretations, she broke off the treatment. In his published account, Freud has the gall to regret her premature departure because it deprived him of the possibility of overcoming her sexual inhibitions sufficiently to enable her to succumb to Herr K.'s advances (and thus render him less prone to object to Herr Bauer's attention's to Frau K.).

A famous case that Freud claimed to have cured, knowing perfectly well that he had not, was that of the 'Wolf Man' (Sergei Pankeev) which Freud published in 1918. Because Pankeev lost his family fortune in Russia, Freud treated him for nothing and provided him with financial assistance during the five years of his analysis. Although Freud claimed to have cured Pankeev's depression and obsessional neurosis, Pankeev was to remain in and out of analytic treatment for many years. He seems to have become something of a psychoanalytic rentier, subsidized financially and supported emotionally by one analyst after another perhaps in the hope that he would not tell his true story to outsiders. However, in the 1970s, he eventually spilled the beans to an Austrian journalist, Karin Obholzer, reporting that his disagreeable symptoms had persisted and that analysis had not particularly helped him.

As a critical reading of the published account of the case makes clear, Freud did not hesitate throughout the course of the analysis to impose his theoretical assumptions on the clinical data. His theory of neurosis demanded a 'primal scene', to provide the sexual trauma necessary to account for Pankeev's symptoms, and Freud found it in a dream which Pankeev remembered from the age of four. Freud's interpretation of this dream provides a telling illustration of the ease with which he would invent aetiological fantasies which were based on his own experiences of childhood and not on those of his patient.

In Pankeev's childhood dream, six white wolves with large tails (actually they were dogs) sat perfectly still in a tree outside his bedroom window. The wolves, Freud told him, were his parents. That they were white was an evident association with bed linen, and their stillness meant the opposite—vigorous copulation. Their large tails, by the same mysterious logic, meant castration. It was clear, declared Freud, that about the age of one, Pankeev from his cot had observed his parents copulating, doggy fashion, on three successive occasions, and he had soiled himself in horrified disgust. Pankeev himself never accepted Freud's explanation: it was, he said, 'terribly far-fetched'. He had no recollection of ever seeing his parents having sex or of soiling himself on such an occasion. In any case, he argued convincingly, it would not have been possible, since no child of his class and background ever slept in a cot in his parents' bedroom. But, of the two people engaged in this analysis, one of them did sleep in his parents' bedroom, did believe he had witnessed the 'primal scene', and did have a traumatic memory of urinating there, and that was not Sergei Pankeev but Sigmund Freud ('That boy will never amount to anything!').

Transference vs relationship

Of all the concepts introduced by Freud during his 'creative illness' (which he referred to as his period of 'splendid isolation'), the one that has had a most profound and lasting influence on the development of psychodynamic therapy is that of 'transference'. 'What do you think of the transference?' Freud demanded during an early exchange with Jung. 'That it is the alpha and omega of psychoanalysis', replied Jung. 'Then you have understood the main thing', said Freud.

Freud introduced the term *transference* to describe the process by which a patient unconsciously transfers on to the person of the analyst feelings and attitudes that were, in fact, possessed by significant people, particularly parents, in the past. This gives rise to the so-called transference relationship between patient and analyst. This has to be distinguished from the *analytic relationship* or the *therapeutic alliance*, which refers to the total relationship between analyst and patient as real people.

Freud came to see transference as an artificially induced neurosis in which patients repeated all the attitudes, assumptions, feelings and modes of relating that they had developed in relation to their parents. This was an insight of the greatest significance. To this day, 'analysis of the transference' is the defining characteristic of all psychodynamic treatment that distinguishes it from other forms of psychotherapy.

Being a somewhat schizoid personality, Freud did not welcome the strong feelings patients often experienced, and expressed, in relation to himself. 'As for the transference', he wrote in 1910, 'it is altogether a curse.' On the face of it, the clinical approach he advocated might seem designed to circumvent such feelings, but, as we shall see, it only served to generate them. 'I cannot advise my colleagues too urgently', wrote Freud, in his 'Recommendations to Physicians Practising Psychoanalysis', 'to model themselves during psychoanalytic treatment on the surgeon, who puts aside all his feelings, even his human sympathy, and concentrates all his mental forces on the single aim of performing the operation as skilfully as possible' (*SE* 12, p.115). He advocated 'emotional coldness' on the part of the analyst, who should be opaque to his patients and, like a mirror, show them nothing but what is shown to him.

Adopting his historical perspective to telling effect, Henri Ellenberger has pointed out that Freud's attitudes to his patients must be understood in the light of what neuropathologists wrote at the end of the nineteenth century about the 'diabolical cleverness' employed by hysterics to deceive their doctor and draw him into their own devious strategies: 'It is as if each rule of Freudian technique was devised to defeat the cunning of these patients', wrote Ellenberger.

One might add that each rule was also devised to strengthen the doctor's position in coercing his patients. The rule that all appointments must be paid for in advance, whether kept or not, prevents the patient from punishing the analyst or resisting the analytic process through absenteeism and non-payment. This also renders the analyst's livelihood more secure and further strengthens his ability to control the patient. By sitting behind patients, out of view, the analyst deprives them of an audience and of the satisfaction of being able to see his reactions. By insisting on analysing the transference, the analyst defeats the hysteric's concealed but always present purpose of seducing him. For this reason, any kind of 'acting out' or physical contact is prohibited, as is social contact outside the therapeutic situation. And because of the hysteric's determination to defeat the analyst by all means at her disposal, even at the cost of remaining ill and socially incapacitated, a cure must never be promised and the patient told that improvement will depend entirely on her own efforts. In this way, the analyst neatly absolves himself of all responsibility for failure.

As we shall see, similar rules apply in Kleinian analysis, where failure to benefit from analysis is attributed to the patient's 'destructive envy' of the 'good breast' proffered by the analyst. Application of these rules by an emotionally cold analyst, going about his business with the objective precision of a surgeon, treating his patients emotional responses to him as being nothing but repetitions from the past, had a number of consequences not always helpful for the patients. To begin with, it meant that any genuine feelings they might be experiencing as adults in the here and now were uniformly discounted. Secondly, Freud's charismatic authority, combined with his insistence that he 'knew' what was going on in their minds had the effect of infantilizing them and resurrecting in them feelings that they had indeed experienced long ago in relation to their parents. Ashamed of such feelings, patients were understandably reluctant to talk about them—a reluctance Freud invariably interpreted as 'resistance' and took as confirmation of his theory of sexual repression.

Most importantly, the whole Freudian technique put patients in a position of extreme emotional vulnerability. Having encouraged them to reveal the most intimate, guilty and embarrassing secrets of their lives, the analyst offered no reassurance, no emotional support, and, above all, no reciprocation, which in any normal human relationship they would have had every right to expect. This, again, deepens patients' sense of helpless dependency on the analyst and increases the strength of their longings for his reassurance and his love.

These criticisms of classic Freudian technique are not new. They were made very cogently in a 'secret diary' kept in 1932 by one of Freud's hitherto most trusted lieutenants, Sándor Ferenzci. Significantly, the diary was suppressed for over fifty years and was published for the first time in a French translation in 1985. In it, Ferenzci frankly acknowledges the feelings of power the analyst can enjoy over 'numbers of helplessly worshipful patients, who admire the analyst unreservedly'; he can prolong their treatment as long as he likes and turn them into lifelong taxpayers. For, however extreme their sufferings and however unsuccessful the treatment, the infantilized patient cannot walk out of the analysis— 'just as it is impossible for a child to run away from home, because, left on its own, it would feel helpless.' He records Freud as saying, 'patients are only riffraff', and that all they were good for was to help the analyst to make a living and to provide material for concocting theories. 'He looms like a god above his poor patient, who has been degraded to the status of a child. We claim that the transference comes from the patient, unaware of the fact that the greater part of what one calls the transference is artificially provoked by this very behaviour.'

In the course of his life, Freud subjected the transference concept to a number of revisions. Perhaps the most important of these was in *Beyond The Pleasure Principle* (1920) where he shifted the emphasis of analytic work away from exploration of unconscious motives to the analysis of the ego's mechanisms of defence. Since unconscious drives were experienced as threats, the ego defended itself against the consequent anxiety by protecting itself behind a battery of defences such as denial, repression, reaction-formation, projection, rationalization, etc. The task of the analyst must be to dismantle these defences and to assist the patient in 'working through' the underlying anxiety, while relating the process to the existence and subsequent removal of neurotic symptoms. The patient was then expected to develop more appropriate defences and to achieve a better adjustment to the issues of life. However, the dismantling of patients' defences could be an extremely painful process, and it had the inevitable consequence of further increasing their emotional vulnerability and their dependence on the analyst.

It was not until publication of *Analysis Terminable and Interminable* in 1937 that Freud finally acknowledged that it was not always possible to terminate an analysis after a definite period with a lasting cure. Some patients had to re-enter analysis from time to time, while others had to continue indefinitely through life. He did not, of course, consider the possibility that this might be because psychoanalysis was ineffective in these cases. On the contrary, it was due to deficiencies in the patient, such as weakness of the ego or to the constitutional power of the unconscious drives, especially of the death instinct. In his posthumous *Outline of Psychoanalysis*, Freud added 'psychic inertia' to the list of defects shared by unresponsive patients, together with a weak capacity for the sublimation of sexual and destructive impulses.

Since Freud's death, the transference concept has undergone many further revisions, and it is true to say that contemporary psychodynamic therapists attribute neurosis less to repressed drives than to a failure on the part of the patient to make satisfactory and lasting human relationships. Analysis of the transference now involves the interpretation of the patient's modes of relating to the analyst in the present. The early origins of these patterns are examined but the main emphasis is on revealing how the patient's difficulties in relating to others are reflected in the analytic relationship. The success of this delicate procedure depends in great measure on the sensitivity of the analyst in shifting the focus of attention between the transference relationship and the real relationship of the 'therapeutic alliance'. We shall be returning to this crucial theme at a later stage.

Inevitably, analysts as well as patients bring unconscious baggage with them when embarking on the analytic encounter. At first Freud assumed that the analyst would, through his own self-analysis or his training analysis, be so aware of the unconscious material he brought with him from the past that he would be incapable of transferring it to his patients. With time and experience, however, Freud and his colleagues acknowledged that this was by no means always the case and it was necessary to monitor the unconscious reactions their patients released in them if they were not to distort the therapeutic alliance in unintended ways. These unconscious projections by the analyst on to the patient make up what Freud called the *countertransference*. Introducing the term in a paper published in 1910, Freud insisted that it was essential for the analyst to recognize his countertransference and overcome it: 'Anyone who fails to produce results in a self-analysis of this kind may at once give up any idea of being able to treat patients by analysis' (1910, pp. 144–45).

Unfortunately, the emphasis placed in recent decades on the importance of analysis of the transference as a means of solving problems of relationship has led to such an extension of the meanings attributed to these useful terms as to render them virtually redundant. Thus, transference has come to refer to the patient's total emotional attitude to the analyst, while countertransference has come to cover the total emotional reaction of the analyst to the patient. The unfortunate consequence of this totalistic application of the terms has been to crowd out the no less important concept—research would indicate that it is more important—of the therapeutic alliance. We shall return to this issue when we consider the implications of 'object relations theory' for psychodynamic therapy.

The ingredients of success

We must conclude that Freud's most extraordinary achievements were neither clinical nor scientific but personal and promotional. With impressive tactical skill he was able to present himself as a fearless searcher after truth, a lonely genius surrounded by lesser men and beset with the hostility of a dismissive, anti-Semitic medical establishment, a selfless scientist of impregnable integrity, totally incapable of fraud or malpractice. Now that this self-serving myth has been torn away, he stands exposed as an unscrupulous clinician, capable of bullying his patients into providing the data he needed to 'prove' his aetiological fantasies, and of generating an extensive literature which used and re-used a tiny number of 'classic' cases with such consumate cunning as to create the illusion of an enormous clinical database.

Yet, for all that, he remains an outstanding historical figure, more famous by far than any of his critics or detractors. How did he do it? Knowing what we now know, how could it be that Freud was destined to become the most celebrated psychological architect of the twentieth century? How could he get away with using a few half-baked bricks and much crumbling mortar to build a fantastic Manhattan of the mind that thousands queued up to enter and secure leases?

The cultural success of psychoanalysis can be understood, as we have already seen, as due to its apparent ability to meet the desire for an all-inclusive explanatory system to replace the religious belief systems which Western society had lost. Freud and Jung were both personally seeking a psychological substitute for their lost religious faith and, far from being alone in this, they articulated the cultural plight of millions, and seemed to provide a solution. Accordingly, Freud did not confine himself to treating neurosis, but strove throughout his life to create a coherent system of ideas capable of explaining the psycho-social functions of art, literature, religion and the traditional institutions of society.

Largely because of the myth Freud created round himself, psychoanalysis was seen as a brilliant scientific achievement that had arisen *de novo* from his own empirical observations. Until the publication of Ellenberger's *Discovery of the Unconscious* in 1970, it was not realized how many of Freud's original discoveries were in fact ideas he had from such luminaries as Darwin, Haeckel, Schopenhauer, Fechner and Nietzsche, as well as Brücke, Meynert, Charcot, Breuer and Fliess. Darwin's vision of psychology as a science based on the biology of instinct was adopted by Freud as his basic premise, while Haeckel's now discredited 'biogenic law' that 'ontogeny recapitulates phylogeny' (that personal development of the individual goes through the same phases as the evolutionary development of the species) was accepted by Freud without question. He used it in *Totem and Taboo* (1913) in order to explain the Oedipus complex as an individual recapitulation of a primordial crime which Freud believed had actually occurred in the ancestral past when a tyrannical Father, ruler of the primal horde, was murdered by his sons.

Schopenhauer's *The World as Will and Idea* had an enormous success in the second half of the nineteenth century and deeply influenced the work of such figures as Wagner, Nietzsche and Thomas Mann, as well as Freud and Jung. What Schopenhauer called the 'Will' was the blind force that prevailed throughout the universe and guided the life of humanity; the 'idea' constituted the conscious realm of phenomena. This was an extension of the distinction made by Kant between the thing-in-itself *(das Ding-an-sich)* and the phenomena to which the thing-in-itself gives rise. Schopenhauer's 'Will', the irrational force which drives us but of which we are largely unaware, consists of two instincts: preservation and sex. Of the two, sex is much stronger: 'Man is incarnate sexual instinct', wrote Schopenhauer, 'since he owes his origin to copulation and the wish of his wishes is to copulate'. Freud's attribution of sex as the central motivating force of the unconscious psyche and his later distinction between the id (the Will') and the ego (the 'idea') are evident transpositions of Schopenhauerian metaphysics into Freudian metapsychology.

But of all the cultural influences helping to shape Freud's thinking, none were greater than the ideas of Friedrich Nietzsche (1844–1900), which permeated the intellectual climate of the 1880s and 90s. Characteristically, Freud attempted to disown Nietzsche's influence, insisting that he developed his theories independently and empirically. He even had the audacity to write condescendingly of Nietzsche as a philosopher 'whose guesses and intuitions often agree in the most astonishing way with the laborious findings of psychoanalysis'! And he makes the ingenuous claim that he had avoided reading Nietzsche for many years so as to keep his mind free of all Nietzschean influences! Even if this were true, it would not have been possible for any educated man of the period to remain in ignorance of Nietzsche's ideas, since they were constantly being quoted and discussed in cafés, newspapers, periodicals and journals throughout the German-speaking world.

One of Nietzsche's aphorisms could have provided the justification of Freud's life: 'Against positivism, which halts at phenomena—"There are facts"—I would say: No, facts are precisely what there are not, only interpretations.' Nietzsche's lifelong emphasis on the unconscious, orgiastic, self-destructive (Dionysian) side of human nature, apparently to the detriment of the calm, conscious, orderly and rational (Apollonian) side, finds echoes in Freud's distinction between primary and secondary process thinking, between the pleasure principle and the reality principle, between the id and the ego.

Like Nietzsche, Freud was to prove an accomplished exponent of the 'uncovering' or 'unmasking' psychology that strips all human phenomena to the lowest common denominator. This trend began with the French moralists of the seventeenth century, achieving its most dazzling expression in *The Maxims* of La Rochefoucauld, with their witty exposure of virtuous pretension as disguised self-advancement. It is unfortunate for the well-being of our culture that one of the most contagious of psychoanalytic prejudices has been that which views human ideals and aspirations as defensive sublimations designed to conceal what is most base in us. Freud's *Civilisation and Its Discontents* (1930) has many parallels with Nietzsche's *Genealogy of Morals* (1887), both being inspired by Diderot's idea that civilisation makes men sick by inhibiting fulfilment of their primordial instincts. Nietzsche's passionate atheism and violent attacks on Christianity may well have encouraged Freud to publish his own iconoclastic views in *Moses and Monotheism* (1939) and *The Future of An Illusion* (1927), in which he dismisses monotheistic religion as the fulfilment of regressive infantile longings for an all-powerful, all-protecting parent.

Though he sought to deny all these influences, Freud nevertheless acknowledged a debt to Gustav Theodor Fechner (1801–1887), from whom he developed his topographical concept of mind, and the concept of mental energy, as well as the principles of pleasure–unpleasure and of repetition. But, on the whole, Freud preferred to annexe ideas without acknowledgement, dress them up in his own impressive terminology, and recycle them as empirical discoveries made on his own couch. Thanks to

Ellenberger, Macmillan, Webster, and others, we know that these came less from Freud's consulting room than from his library. Freud's achievement was to weave these ideas into a new synthesis, devising new rituals for the treatment of neurotic disorders via the analytic situation, the analytic relationship, and the analysis of ego defences and the transference.

That so many of the root ideas of psychoanalysis were current in the culture of Freud's time goes a long way to explain the readiness with which psychoanalytic doctrines were eventually accepted. One area in which psychoanalysts continue to claim primacy for Freud's achievement is in his fearless introduction of novel sexual theories at a time when discussion of anything sexual was considered 'taboo'. But this again is not the case. It is true that there existed a dread of venereal infection, especially syphilis, which inhibited open discussion of sexual topics in polite society, but this does not mean that sex was a taboo subject in intellectual, particularly medical, circles, as is evidenced by the wide circulation and discussion of books by a new breed of sexologists such as Krafft-Ebing (1840–1902), who published his *Psychopathia Sexualis* in 1886; Magnus Hirschfeldt (1864–1935), who founded the Scientific Humanitarian Committee to defend the rights of homosexuals in 1898; and Henry Havelock Ellis (1859–1939), who published his monumental *Studies in the Psychology of Sex* in seven volumes between 1898 and 1928.

Freud's success in making psychoanalytic ideas accessible to a huge international constituency was due to his undoubted brilliance as a writer. Over the years he developed a wonderfully patrician literary style which lent his utterances great authority; and, as an extempore lecturer, speaking for hours without notes, he was unsurpassed. When he presented a case history, he described the unconscious processes responsible for its symptomatology so convincingly that few members of his audience even suspected that what they were being fed was a highly inventive series of speculations. And those who did suspect often abandoned their disbelief by the time Freud brought his discourse to a close.

His technique, both as writer and lecturer, was to begin with a beguiling show of tentativeness, designed to lull the reader into a sense of being led through dense thickets of complex material by an open-minded guide. Anticipating every possible objection he was careful to disarm each in turn. Then, very gently, he proceeded to persuade his audience to accept as firmly established what had been only tentatively suggested. And, like his hero Sherlock Holmes, formulate the case and present his conclusions in a manner so convincing as to make them seem the only possible deductions from the facts.

Above all psychoanalytic writers he had *Sprachgefühl* (feeling for language) and few were surprised when he received the Goethe prize for Literature in 1930. He admired Shakespeare, Goethe, Schiller, Heine, and the Greek tragedians, whom he called 'his masters', and it is possible that had he devoted his life to literature instead of psychoanalysis he could have been an important creative writer. It is perhaps because of Freud's literary gifts that psychoanalysis is closer to fiction than to science. In an interview with the Italian author Giovanni Papini in 1934, Freud said: 'Though I have the appearance of a scientist, I was and am a poet and novelist.' Bilingual commentators say that something of the high literary merit of the German originals is irretrievably lost in translation, but Freud is, nevertheless, always a pleasure to read in English. So lucid and persuasive is his prose that it possesses instant credibility. Even though Freud invariably preferred arcane explanations to obvious ones, he somehow manages to make one accept his preferences as yet further examples of the percipience and profundity of his thinking

Why was Freud so casual with the truth and so willing to doctor his facts? Was it entirely due to overweening ambition and an obsessive determination to succeed? Not entirely. One of Freud's severest critics, Richard Webster, offers the most charitable explanation: he maintains that Freud was totally convinced of the validity of his theories and genuinely believed that psychoanalysis would make so great a contribution to the relief of suffering in the world that the matter of providing evidence to substantiate his beliefs seemed trivial by comparison and wasteful of his energies. If this is so, then Freud is similar to many other charismatic leaders of esoteric movements, whose appeal to their followers lies in the total conviction with which they express their views.

The charismatic guru

In his book *Feet of Clay* (1996), Anthony Storr had no hesitation in classifying Freud as a guru (a Sanskrit term meaning both 'weighty' and 'one who brings light out of darkness'; in India it is used to designate a Hindu or Sikh religious teacher). In this fascinating study, Storr characterized gurus as people who believe they have been granted some special, life-transforming insight. This usually comes to them at some time in their thirties or forties and typically follows a period of mental or physical illness (which has variously been described as a 'mid-life crisis', a 'creative illness' or 'dark night of the soul'). The Eureka experience may come on gradually or like a thunderbolt in the manner of a religious conversion, a scientific discovery or the intact delusional system of a psychotic illness. As a result, the guru becomes convinced that he has discovered 'the truth', and this conviction, as well as the passion with which he proclaims it, gives him the charisma which makes him attractive to potential followers. Good looks and the ability to speak fluently in public are invaluable additional assets.

In a study published by John Price and myself in the same year as Storr's book appeared, we described charismatic leaders, based on our reading of the available literature, as possessing personal characteristics that would readily satisfy the internationally recognized psychiatric diagnostic criteria of 'borderline', 'schizoid', 'schizotypal' or 'paranoid' personality disorders. Of these, Freud would most readily fit in to the schizoid category; as for that matter would Jung. Freud, as we have noted, had no great opinion of humanity, and throughout his life he preferred correspondence to actual meetings with people. In *An Autobiographical Study* (1925), Freud confines himself to the development of his ideas; he hardly mentions his relations with other people. This is in line with his theoretical focus on drives, their sublimation and repression within the individual, and with his lack of interest in 'object relations', which were to preoccupy the 'neo-Freudians' who came after him.

As Storr pointed out, gurus are more interested in what goes on in their minds than they are in their relationships with others; and being of an authoritarian, anti-democratic disposition, they tend to attract followers rather than friends—their relations with followers being based not on fellowship but on dominance. Accordingly, Freud maintained his ascendancy over other psychoanalysts by keeping his distance from them, while at the same time demanding their complete loyalty and love. Gurus require disciples as much as disciples need a guru, for the guru's conviction in the truth of his message is not always as absolute as it appears, and his confidence requires the constant boost that followers can bring. For this reason, gurus are extremely intolerant of criticism, feeling that anything less than total agreement with their views is equivalent to overt hostility. It was Freud's dogmatic certainty, combined with his refusal to tolerate dissent, that drove unsycophantic colleagues away from him and bound the rest to him with hoops of steel. His insistence that sexuality was the causal factor in every case of hysteria, for example, destroyed his collaboration with Breuer, and guaranteed the eventual estrangement between himself and Jung.

Psychoanalysis thus demonstrates many of the features of that complex relationship between love, power and submission which is characteristic of all messianic movements. Freud's somewhat masochistic submission earlier in life to men such as Brücke, Breuer and Fliess was the reverse of the dominance he later exerted over disciples like Jones, Ferenczi and Rank. Paul Roazen, that perceptive historian of psychoanalytic vicissitudes, has described how many of Freud's disciples and patients, hungry for his love, so identified with him as to mimic his verbal and physical mannerisms. Hans Sachs, for example, became obsessional about catching railway trains in the same way as Freud, while Theodor Reik adopted Freud's manner of smoking cigars, his style of writing and talking, and grew an identical beard. For them Freud came to represent what Jung was to call an archetype—the archetype of the sage, prophet, healer and, ultimately, the wise old man. But what kept all Freud's followers in line was the fear of being perceived as deviant or doctrinally unsound, for the consequences of Freud's excommunication for heresy could, as we shall see, be terrible indeed.

With Freud there was always a tendency for enmity to follow friendship. This happened not only in his relations with Meynert, Breuer and Fliess, but with Jung, Adler, Stekel, and other colleagues who were at one time close to him. Alfred Adler (1870–1937), a Viennese physician, was one of the first disciples to be attracted to Freud, and he remained active in Freud's psychoanalytic circle until differences between them brought about his departure in 1911. Like Jung, Adler came to disagree with the exclusive emphasis Freud placed on sexual development in the aetiology of neurosis, and became increasingly convinced that social instincts, and compensatory power strivings, were more fundamental motivations than sexuality.

As will become clear in the next chapter and in Volume 2, the intellectual differences that arose between the pioneers of psychoanalysis were invariably related to their personal biographies. Disagreements over the importance of the Oedipus complex is a case in point. Whereas Freud's mother had been a beautiful young woman who lavished love and attention on him, Jung's mother, as we shall see, was a homely soul who was prone to attacks of depression, which caused her to spend at least one long period in hospital during her son's early childhood. Freud's concept of the Oedipus complex and its central role in human development grew directly out of his fantasies about his own childhood experience. That neither Jung nor Adler accepted the universality of the Oedipus complex was due to their quite different childhood circumstances. Events in Adler's early history caused him to place great emphasis on the developmental influence of birth order in siblings, and on the individual's need to compensate for early feelings of inferiority, while Jung's sense of maternal deprivation, and a religious crisis experienced during adolescence in relation to his father, caused him to turn inwards and seek spiritual security within himself.

But to Freud, these dissidents were intolerable, and it was in order to protect him from them that Ernest Jones proposed in 1913 that a secret committee should be formed of Freud's most loyal adherents to act as a kind of Praetorian Guard. The objective of this group of intellectual heavies, which we might call the 'Freud Squad', was to engineer the ejection of Jung from the International Psychoanalytic Association, to protect Freud from heretics, and to police the theoretical purity of psychoanalysis.

Freud took to the idea at once, for it offered him some hope that his work might survive after his death: 'I was so uneasy about what the human rabble would make out of it when I was no longer alive', he later recalled. The secret committee was inaugurated on May 25th that year in Freud's consulting room at Bergasse 19 and consisted of Ernest Jones,

Sándor Ferenzci, Max Eitingen, Hans Sachs, Otto Rank and Karl Abraham, as well as Freud himself. Freud presented each of them with an ancient intaglio from his collection of antiquities, which they had mounted on gold rings and wore as pledges of eternal brotherhood. Freud's was incised with the head of Jupiter! All this was done behind Jung's back and while he was still President of the International Association.

It was that summer of 1913 that Freud wrote *Totem and Taboo*, perhaps his most fantastic and controversial book, which demonstrated the extent to which he conceived family dynamics to be based on conflict. Before civilization began, so Freud's fantasy ran, an all-powerful father had possessed all the women of the tribe. His sons eventually banded together, killed him, and ceremonially ate his body. The brothers then quarrel among themselves, and out of remorse for their patricide, decide to accept their father's prohibition against incest. In his secret committee, Freud was, apparently without realizing it, setting up a similar situation: it was as if he were unconsciously inviting its members to kill him and quarrel among themselves. Though Freud survived until 1939, serious tensions certainly developed between members of the committee. Ferenzci and Rank eventually rebelled, and suffered the inevitable excommunication.

The Freudian legacy

What then may we conclude about the consequences of Freud's contribution to psychotherapy and to our culture? The debate about this will continue for a long time to come, some maintaining that he liberated us from sexual inhibition and prudery, others that he seriously eroded the ethical codes of self-discipline and social responsibility on which Western society has hitherto depended. The idea that Freud was the first to stress the importance of sex in neurotic aetiology at a time when all mention of sex was prohibited is, as we have already seen, part of the Freudian legend. As already noted, at the turn of the century Vienna was awash with sexual theorizing. The works of Moritz Benedikt, Richard von Krafft-Ebing, Otto Weininger, Havelock Ellis and Magnus Hirschfeldt were well known and a source of much discussion in intellectual circles at the time. But in the wider, less sophisticated culture there was still much sexual guilt and shame, against which the rising influence of psychoanalysis had to struggle. The eventual triumph of Freudian theory, however, contributed to a cultural obsession with sex—to the exaggerated emphasis on the importance of a satisfied sexual appetite for human happiness; to the salacious public interest, inflamed by media titillation, in the private sexual life of all celebrities; and to the uncritical acceptance of the idea that most human actions, however altruistic, are sexually motivated. By setting himself up as the unmasker of hypocrisy and pretension, advocating a systematic exposure of the mechanisms people use to defend themselves against their real desires, Freud generated the belief that peoples' true motives are always less creditable than they seem, and that their actions are less inspired by public-spirited ideals than driven by selfish, greedy, aggressive, destructive and lustful passions.

This jaded view of human nature, which has been promoted so enthusiastically by the media, has had unfortunate consequences for both the private and the public domains of contemporary existence. It has led to that seamy atmosphere of suspicion and distrust that would assert that anyone who delights in the company of children must be a paedophile. It has brought us to the sad point where fathers are fearful of expressing love for their daughters lest it be seized on as 'evidence' of incest or abuse; doctors are fearful of offering physical comfort to distressed patients by putting an arm round their shoulder or holding their hand lest this be construed as an attempt at seduction; and employers are fearful of complimenting their employees on their appearance lest it exposes them to an accusation of sexual harassment. It is of course true that children are sometimes abused, patients seduced or young people are sexually harassed but, when interest in these matters becomes exaggerated or obsessive, it can have most unhappy consequences for the human exchanges of ordinary social life.

Perhaps Freud's major bequest to his followers was that form of convincing yet spurious authority which Robin Dawes (1994) has called the 'myth of expertise'—the self-assumed justification to claim special knowledge about patients, which is not only unavailable to less qualified practitioners but also inaccessible to the patients themselves. Taking Freud as their model, generations of psychoanalysts, therapists and social workers have felt justified in making assumptions on theoretical grounds as to the nature of the unconscious and repressed material responsible for making people ill, and, in the name of therapy, 'helping' their clients to 'remember'. The philosopher Isaiah Berlin foresaw this danger many years ago. To assume that one knows someone better than they know themselves, and to believe that one is justified in overriding their protests in the interests of their own good, can readily become a justification to 'bully, oppress, torture them in the name, and on behalf, of their "real" selves'.

Freud repeatedly reassured his readers and audiences that he had abandoned hypnosis and the use of suggestion in the early 1890s, preferring to allow his patients, through their free associations, to lead him, like an explorer without a map, through the jungle of their unconscious memories to the sexual traumata at the root of their disorder. As a result, psychoanalysts, and indeed all psychodynamic therapists, have tended grossly to underestimate the power of suggestion in therapy, and have too uncritically accepted the belief that true memories can be unearthed, uncontaminated by the prejudices and preoccupations of the practitioner. The many terrible instances of injustice that have resulted from faith in the 'recovered memory syndrome' have shown the extent to which the human psyche is vulnerable to suggestion. As research has overwhelmingly demonstrated, it is evident that psychotherapy is still too primitive a discipline to be able to claim that it can use signs, symptoms and symbols to detect the existence of unconscious events and repressed memories of which patients declare they know nothing. At the present state of knowledge, a therapist who does this automatically stands convicted of professional malpractice.

It would hardly be fair, however, to blame Freud for all the ills that have overtaken Western society in the twentieth century. The sociologists and political ideologues must take their share of the blame. Moreover, much social advocacy and legislation has been based on misinterpretations of Freud's views. The 'liberation philosophy' of the 1960s, for example, was promoted by media pundits who, having absorbed a distorted version of Freudian theory, genuinely believed we had such certain knowledge of human nature as to justify changing laws and institutions so radically as to liberate people from social constraint and set them free to seek their individual self-fulfilment, uninhibited by the repressive machinery of the State. Unfortunately, the intellectual steam driving the '60s revolution was generated by the wholly erroneous idea that Freud had proved sexual repression to be the cause of all social ills.

What Freud actually maintained, on the contrary, was that the suppression and sublimation of instinctual forces into socially responsible modes of behaviour actually made civilization possible. Now that the truth of this realization is beginning to dawn, the time has passed when it is possible to do much to rectify the damage. The central flaw in Freud's theorizing and his promotion of 'an ethical disease among the many' is the fact that he set himself the goal of creating a science of human nature before the time for such an achievement had arrived, and that he then used all his skill as a communicator to persuade the world that he had created it. Too many influential people took him at his word. We shall continue to suffer the consequences of this misfortune far into the twenty-first century.

But has no good come out of what Richard Webster calls this 'complex pseudo-science which should be recognized as one of the great follies of Western civilization'? Although he did not always practise what he preached, Freud's advocacy of an objective, nonjudgemental attitude to patients and their problems contributed to the development of a more tolerant and humane approach to neurosis and to sexual deviation. His influence helped to persuade the medical profession, as well as the public at large, that these were essentially developmental disorders and not the result of hereditary 'taints', constitutional 'degeneration' or inherent wickedness. By introducing the formal ritual of the psychoanalytic '50-minute hour', he established the fundamental psychotherapeutic principle of providing what no other human relationship provides—a safe environment in which a qualified professional gives individual patients undivided and sympathetic attention, getting to know them intimately without judging or rejecting them, but respecting their essential humanity.

The majority of people who seek psychotherapeutic help feel they have seldom, if ever, been accepted or valued for what they are. To be able to reveal their social anxieties, personal doubts and feelings of low self-esteem to another human being not only enables them to objectify their troubles and find solutions to them but to embark on a process of self-discovery and self-affirmation which is itself experienced as healing. In all forms of mental distress the crucial remedy is to find oneself accepted, understood, reaffirmed and valued as a member of the human race. Insofar as Freud was responsible for rediscovering this therapeutic principle and making it available to vulnerable people in our society we must be forever in his debt.

3
ANALYTICAL PSYCHOLOGY
AND CARL GUSTAV JUNG (1875-961)

A widely accepted view of Jung is that of a woolly-minded defector who betrayed the strict scientific principles of psychoanalysis in order to found a mystical cult of his own. This distortion, which started with Freud and his inner circle, has proved remarkably resilient, resurfacing in the writings of Richard Noll and Frank McLynn. The truth is very different. As will become clear, the basic hypotheses postulated by Jung during and after his break with Freud have stood the test of time better than those of his erstwhile mentor. For example, Jung's theory of 'archetypes' making up the 'collective unconscious' of a phylogenetically endowed psyche, his ideas about psychopathology and the adaptive nature of psychiatric symptoms find close parallels in the ideas current in contemporary evolutionary psychiatry.

'Father and son'

Jung went to Vienna to meet Freud for the first time in March 1907. They were so captivated by one another that they talked without stopping for thirteen hours. Freud was 50 and still struggling to establish his reputation as the founder of psychoanalysis; Jung was 31, a promising psychiatrist on the great Eugen Bleuler's staff at the Burghölzli Hospital in Zurich, who had already achieved recognition through his demonstration of the existence of unconscious complexes through his use of the word association test, originally devised by the English physicist Sir Francis Galton. Following this first encounter, an intense friendship developed between Jung and Freud which lasted—mostly through letters—for six years.

On the face of it this was an odd relationship between two men of different age, character and background. Jung, a rural Protestant, son of a Swiss pastor, conventionally educated, was steeped in theology and Romantic idealism; while Freud, an urban Jew, was educated in a progressive tradition that led him naturally into science and atheism. Jung's published work on the association test and his book *The Psychology of*

Dementia Praecox (1906), as well as his position as Bleuler's second-in-command at the Burghölzli, meant that he was both well known and highly regarded in international psychiatric circles. Freud, on the other hand, was a much more controversial figure because of his ideas on the polymorphous perversity of infants and the sexual aetiology of neurosis. Of the two, Jung was at that time considered the better scientist. For Jung to throw in his lot with Freud was personally and professionally risky and, as we shall see, he was destined to emerge from the relationship psychologically scarred, his reputation in tatters.

What drew them to one another? From the start, it was clear that each felt the other could help further his professional ambitions; but gradually both began to find fulfilment of deeper personal needs in their burgeoning friendship. Freud's closest associates in Vienna quickly became envious of the affectionate attention he lavished on Jung and resented the special relationship that was growing up between them. Freud was irritated by this reaction, which he regarded as the sort of petty-mindedness typical of the second-rate individuals who made up his small Viennese clique. Jung, by contrast, so supremely able and well placed in the psychiatric world, had the added advantages, in Freud's view, of being neither Jewish nor Viennese. Freud hoped that his new ally might rescue psychoanalysis from the ever-present threat of anti-Semitic hostility, draw it out of its parochial obscurity, and gain for it a place on the international stage.

From their very first meeting, Jung was fascinated by Freud: 'Freud was the first man of real importance I had encountered', he wrote in his memoir *Memories, Dreams, Reflections*:

> In my experience up to that time, no one else could compare with him. There was nothing the least trivial in his attitude. I found him extremely intelligent, shrewd and altogether remarkable. And yet my first impressions of him remained somewhat tangled; I could not make him out. …
>
> What he said about his sexual theory impressed me. Nevertheless, his words could not remove my hesitations and doubts. I tried to advance these reservations of mine on several occasions, but each time he would attribute them to my lack of experience. Freud was right; in those days I had not enough experience to support my objections. I could see that his sexual theory was enormously important to him, both personally and philosophically When he spoke of it, his tone became urgent, almost anxious,

and all signs of his normally critical and sceptical manner vanished. A strange, deeply moved expression came over his face, the cause of which I was at a loss to understand (*MDR*, pp. 146–147).

As Jung saw it, Freud, who made no secret of his atheism, had turned his sexual theory into a pseudo-religious dogma: in place of Yahweh, whom he had lost, he substituted another daemonic force: 'sexual libido', a *deus absconditus*, a numinous principle which Freud claimed as scientific and removed from all religious taint.

Two days after their first encounter, Jung returned for a second meeting with Freud, this time bringing with him another young Swiss psychiatrist, Ludwig Binswanger. Freud asked them both about the dreams they had had the night before, and proceeded to interpret Jung's dream as involving a wish to dethrone him and take his place. The mood of the meeting was, however, extremely congenial: 'Freud's dislike of all formality and ceremony,' recorded Binswanger afterwards, 'his personal charm, simplicity, natural openness and kindness, and not least his humour, left no room for constraint. And yet one could not for a moment deny the impression of greatness and dignity that emanated from him. To me it was a pleasure, albeit somewhat sceptical, to see the enthusiasm and confidence with which Freud responded to Jung, in whom he immediately saw his scientific "son and heir" '.

Jung, evidently pleased by the esteem in which Freud held him, was drawn to his distinguished older colleague as to a mentor whom fate had provided at a critical moment in his career. To Jung, Freud represented the intellectually courageous father that his own timid, reticent and self-doubting father could never have been. In contrast to the rather tragic, spiritually inadequate country pastor, who had suffered the catastrophe of losing his faith, Freud was a towering figure who spoke with total conviction out of his hard-won experience. Jung was happy to accept the subordinate position in their relationship, for, as he acknowledged, he still had much to learn. Soon after their first meeting, he wrote to Freud: 'Let me enjoy your friendship not as one between equals but as that of father and son.' While in a letter to Jung, Freud wrote of his 'long years of honourable but painful solitude' and of the 'serene certainty which finally took possession of me and bade me wait until a voice from the unknown multitude should answer mine. That voice was yours.'

If Jung needed a father, Freud needed a son whom he considered worthy to inherit his kingdom and continue his rule. Unfortunately, this was not the sort of relationship that could last. On his side, Freud was not particularly keen to see his 'son' grow up: he would have preferred a devoted disciple willing to accept his doctrines and respect his authority without reservation. For several years, he continued to make fulsome allusions to Jung's brilliance as a psychoanalyst and to his crucial importance for the future of the movement. This embarrassed Jung because, as he increasingly realized, he would never be able to uphold Freud's ideas in their entirety. Nevertheless, in accordance with Freud's wishes, he allowed himself to become the first President of the International Psychoanalytic Association, and chief editor of the first psychoanalytic journal, the *Jahrbuch*.

What Jung really needed was a father-figure whom he could admire sufficiently to overcome the spiritual doubts that had tormented him since childhood, discover his own masculine authority, and establish himself as a major figure in the world of psychiatry. Freud, it is true, was as much caught up in a father–son complex as Jung, but with the added fact that in Freud's personal myth the son was equated with thrusting ascendancy and the father with inexorable decline. As a consequence, as is evidenced by Freud's interpretation of Jung's first dream, he readily detected the parricide in Jung, and it deeply upset him—to the extent that he fainted on two separate occasions when Jung happened to mention to him the subject of death.

Schism: the son goes his own way

During the years of their association, Jung was able to make significant contributions to psychoanalytic theory and practice. Not only did his word association experiments provide hard empirical evidence for the existence and power of unconscious complexes, but also his work with schizophrenics at the Burghölzli carried psychoanalytic concepts into areas beyond Freud's reach. In addition, Jung infected Freud with an enthusiasm for the study of mythology and comparative religion, though not, as it turned out, with happy consequences, for the conclusions that both men drew from these studies were explosively at variance.

As time passed, Jung's differences with Freud became harder to conceal. Two of Freud's basic assumptions were unacceptable to him: that human motivation is exclusively sexual, and that the unconscious mind is entirely personal and peculiar to the individual. Jung found these and other aspects of Freud's thinking reductionist and narrow. Instead of conceiving psychic energy (or *libido* as Freud called it) as wholly sexual, Jung preferred to think of it as a more generalized 'life force', of which sexuality was but one mode of expression. Moreover, beneath the personal unconscious of repressed wishes and traumatic memories posited by Freud, Jung believed there lay a deeper and more important phylogenetic (evolved) layer that he was to call the *collective unconscious,* which contained the entire psychic potential of mankind. The existence of this ancient basis of mind had first been hinted to him as a child when he realized that there were things in his dreams that came from somewhere beyond himself. He believed that the reality of the collective unconscious was confirmed when he and his colleagues studied the delusions and hallucinations of schizophrenic patients and found them to contain symbols and images that also occurred in myths and fairy tales all over the world. He concluded that there must exist a dynamic psychic layer, common to all humanity, on the basis of which each individual builds his or her private experience of life.

Whenever Jung attempted to express these ideas to Freud, however, they were firmly discounted and attributed either to youthful inexperience or to 'resistance'. 'Don't deviate too far from me when you are really so close to me, for if you do, we may one day be played off against one another,' Freud prophetically admonished him, adding a sinister little threat: 'My inclination is to treat those colleagues who offer resistance exactly as we would treat patients in the same situation'! Jung was irked by such a condescending attempt at intimidation and a row became unavoidable. It was heralded in 1911 by the publication of the first part of Jung's *Transformations and Symbols of the Libido*. As if warning Freud of the heresies to come, Jung wrote to him saying 'It is a risky business for an egg to be cleverer than the hen. Still what is in the hen must find the courage to creep out.'

The row finally erupted in 1912 with the publication of Part Two of *Transformations*.

This time Jung wrote to Freud quoting Zarathustra: 'One repays a teacher badly if one remains only a pupil.' In this work and in a series of lectures given in New York in September 1912, Jung spelled out the heretical view that libido was a much wider concept than Freud allowed and that it could appear in 'crystallized' form in the universal symbols or 'primordial images' apparent in the myths of humanity. Jung drew special attention to the myth of the hero, interpreting the recurrent theme of his fight with a dragon-monster as the struggle of the adolescent ego for deliverance from the mother. This led Jung to interpretations of the Oedipus complex and the incest taboo that were very different from those proposed by Freud. In Jung's view, a child became attached to his mother not because she was the object of incestuous passion, as Freud maintained, but because she was the provider of love and care—a view that anticipated the theoretical revolution wrought some forty years later by the British psychoanalyst and psychiatrist John Bowlby.

Publication of these views provoked a major rift with Freud that resulted in the formal termination of their relationship early in 1913. Jung resigned his Presidency of the Association, his editorship of the *Jahrbuch*, his lectureship at the University of Zurich, and withdrew altogether from the psychoanalytic movement. He was now entirely on his own.

Given the characteristics of both men, it was inevitable that their intellectual union would end in divorce. To Jung, the ultimate goal in life was to realize one's potential, follow one's own vision of the truth, and become as complete a human being as one's personal circumstances would allow (i.e., to achieve what he was later to call the goal of *individuation*). He had to go his own way. It was Freud's misfortune that his intolerance of dissent meant that he often ended up by provoking it: he was a strange mixture of autocrat and masochist. The loss of Jung was a tragic blow to him and it took him a long time to get over it, but once it had happened, there could be no going back and, henceforth, he regarded Jung as both a traitor and an implacable enemy. Early on, he had confessed to Jung that his emotional life demanded the existence of an intimate friend and a hated enemy and that, not infrequently, both coincided in the same person. This pattern was apparent in his childhood relationship with his nephew John (who happened to be his own age), and in his relationship with Wilhelm Fliess. A similar fate overtook his friendships with Breuer,

Meynert, Adler, Stekel, Silberer, Tausk and Wilhelm Reich. Such was the power of Freud's personal charisma that his anathema could have appalling consequences for the excommunicant: Reich, for example, developed a psychotic illness, from which he recovered only temporarily, while Silberer and Tausk eventually committed suicide.

Confrontation with the unconscious

For Jung the disaster was almost as dire: he fell into a protracted 'state of disorientation', at times verging on psychosis, which lasted four or five years. Although profoundly disturbing—to his family no less than to himself—this proved to be a period of intense creativity that Jung referred to as his 'confrontation with the unconscious', and Ellenberger has diagnosed as a further, well-documented example of a 'creative illness'.

It is interesting that Jung suffered his creative illness at an identical period of his life to Freud, between the ages of 38 and 43, though in Jung's case the symptoms were more incapacitating and their origins more profound. Ellenberger describes the illness as being prone to strike after a time of intense intellectual activity and it resembles a neurosis or, in severe cases, a psychosis. Still struggling with the issues that were a prelude to the condition, the sufferer is convinced that he is beyond outside help, becomes socially isolated, and turns deeper into himself. As with Jung, the disturbance can last four or five years. When recovery sets in, it occurs spontaneously and is associated with euphoria and a transformation of the personality. The subject feels that he has gained insight into important truths and believes that he has a duty to share these with the world.

At times the disturbance was so severe as to bring Juang to the edge of madness. He played in his garden like a child, heard voices in his head, walked about holding conversations with imaginary figures and, during one episode, believed his house to be crowded with the spirits of the dead. However, he did not lose touch with reality altogether, and it is a measure of his unusual quality that he regarded this disaster as if it were an experiment being performed on himself. To be a psychiatrist in the grip of a breakdown gave him an opportunity for research! He could study the whole experience at first hand and use it to help his patients:

This idea—that I was committing myself to a dangerous enterprise not for myself alone, but also for the sake of my patients—helped me over several critical phases. ... It is, of course, ironical that I, a psychiatrist, should at almost every step in my experiment have run into the same psychic material which is the stuff of psychosis and is found in the insane. This is the fund of unconscious images which fatally confuse the mental patient. But it is also the matrix of a mythopoeic imagination which has vanished from our rational age (*MDR*, pp. 172, 181).

There are close parallels between Jung's experience and anthropological descriptions of the initiatory illness passed through by Siberian, African and North American shamans. The Tungus noun *saman* means 'one who is excited, moved, raised'. As a verb, it means 'to know in an ecstatic manner'. Ethnological studies reveal the majority of shamans to be borderline personalities if not, on occasion, frankly schizophrenic. As with all charismatic leaders and gurus, their influence arises from the uncanny, hypnotic power of their personalities, and their apparent ability to put themselves in close touch with the unconscious and articulate its contents in a way that convinces their followers that they are inspired.

Jung was to look back on the years of his 'confrontation with the unconscious' as the most important of his life: 'In them everything essential was decided (*MDR*, p. 191).

They provided him with the basis of the psychotherapeutic discipline that bears his name. 'It all began then; the later details are only supplements and clarifications of the material that burst from the unconscious, and at first swamped me. It was the *prima materia* for a lifetime's work' (*MDR*, p. 191). Much of this material, which he recorded in his *Liber Novum,* the so-called *Red Book,* caused a publishing sensation when it eventually saw the light of day in 2009.

If Jung was not a guru before his break with Freud, he was now to become one, and following publication of his first major work in which he announced his new insights, *Psychological Types* (1921), people flocked to Zurich from other continental countries, from Britain and from North America to be analysed by him. Some returned whence they came, but many, especially women, stayed to join the ranks of the entourage surrounding Jung, known to local wits as the *Jungfrauen.*

The inner life of a lonely child

Jung shared many of the characteristics common to gurus. In addition to the shamanic initiation induced by his creative illness, he experienced himself as a solitary, even when surrounded by his family and admiring followers, and placed greater emphasis on his inner life of dreams, fantasies and ideas than on his relationships and social encounters. This pattern became established early in childhood. An only child for the first nine years of his life (his sister Gertrud was born in 1884), he withdrew into himself because of the 'unbreatheable' home atmosphere of 'death, melancholy and unease', caused by the unhappy state of his parents' marriage.

His mother was an uncanny, at times witch-like figure, whom he loved, admired and feared. Emotionally unstable, she spent several months in hospital, apparently for treatment of a depressive illness, when Carl was three, and this enforced separation at a critical stage in his development seems to have affected Jung for the rest of his life. As John Bowlby was later to demonstrate, the despair displayed by young children on the loss of their mother is a normal response to frustration of their absolute need for her presence. Although children usually manage to survive this trauma it is often at the cost of developing a defensive attitude of emotional detachment, and by becoming self-absorbed and self-reliant to an unusual degree. Typically, they are left with lasting doubts about their capacity to elicit care and affection. They also tend to become rather odd and aloof in manner, which does not endear them to others.

Although Carl was cared for by an aunt and a young maid while his mother was away, he recalled being 'deeply troubled' by her absence: he suffered from nervous eczema and had terrifying dreams. 'From then on,' he says, 'I always felt mistrustful when the word "love" was spoken. The feeling I associated with "woman" was for a long time that of innate unreliability' (*MDR*, p. 23). Jung's later reputation as a womanizer was probably in part due to his need to find 'safety in numbers'.

His father Paul, a pastor in the Swiss Reformed Church, was a gentle, tolerant man, but Carl experienced him as powerless and emotionally immature. Quite early in his ministry, Paul Jung seems to have lost his faith, but, lacking any alternative source of income, felt compelled to persevere with his parish duties. Carl found this enforced hypocrisy extremely embarrassing, especially when he had to bear the discomfort of hearing his father preach on Sundays. Inevitably, when Paul Jung prepared his son for confirmation it was a disaster: it had the effect of alienating Carl from the church forever, and starting him on a lifelong quest to find a spiritually satisfying substitute. Whenever Carl attempted to discuss his religious doubts, his father behaved much as Freud was to behave when his younger colleague attempted to express reservations about the sexual theory: both told him to stop questioning and *believe*. This was never acceptable to Jung, who had to *know* (that is, discover the truth for himself).

At school he was unhappy because his somewhat schizoid (withdrawn, aloof, self-absorbed) manner made him unpopular, and his sense of personal singularity was aggravated when a master accused him of plagiarizing an essay he had written with meticulous care. For a long period he dropped out of school altogether by dint of producing fainting spells after a blow to the head. He spent as much time as he could on his own: 'I remained alone with my thoughts. On the whole I liked that best. I played alone, day-dreamed or strolled in the woods alone, and had a secret world of my own' (*MDR*, p. 58).

This secret world compensated for his isolation. The fantasies and rituals common to childhood assumed a heightened intensity for him, and they influenced the rest of his life. For example, his adult delight in studying alone in a tower that he built as a retreat for himself at Bollingen on the upper lake of Zurich was anticipated by a childhood ritual in which he tended a manikin in a pencil box hidden in the attic of his parents' house. Each time he visited the manikin he presented him with a scroll written in a secret language to provide him with a library for his private study. This gave Carl a deep feeling of security: 'No one could discover my secret and destroy it. I felt safe, and the tormenting sense of being at odds with myself was gone' (*MDR*, p. 34).

But not all his secret experiences were agreeable. When he was three or four he had a terrifying dream of an enormous phallic god erect on a throne in an underground cave, from which he deduced that there were more sinister aspects to God than the meek, sexless image of Christ purveyed by the church. This understanding was confirmed by a later vision of God defecating on His cathedral at Basel and smashing in the roof with an enormous turd. This indicated that God had no greater opinion of His church than Carl had. Such experiences convinced him that he had an inner relationship to God which was denied to his spiritually bereft father.

A favourite fantasy with which he entertained himself during the long walk to school was of a fortified citadel with a tall keep, which contained a wonderful secret that he alone knew. Inside the tower was a copper column which extracted a 'spiritual essence' from the atmosphere and drew it down into the cellar, where there was a laboratory in which Carl transformed the airy substance into gold. This seems to have been an early prefiguration of his adult preoccupation with alchemy.

The need to create a citadel in which to hide from the world is characteristic of people with a schizoid disposition. Within his own defensive fortifications, Carl experienced himself as made up of two separate personalities, which he referred to as 'No. 1' and 'No. 2' respectively. No. 1 was the son of his parents who went to school and coped with life as well as he could, while No. 2 was much older, remote from the world of human society, but close to nature and animals, to dreams, and to God. As a psychiatrist Jung formed the opinion that these two personalities were not unique to himself but present in everyone and he called them the ego and the Self. He believed that the play and counter-play between them constituted the central dynamic of personality development. Throughout his adolescence, Carl experienced the Self as God-like and his commitment to this internal 'other' took precedence over all outer relationships. He did not feel himself to be among people, but alone with God.

It is against this background that Jung's 'confrontation with the unconscious' between 1913 and 1918 had to be understood. Having no faith in orthodox Christianity, and having lost faith in Freudian psychoanalysis, he turned to the 'God within' and to the guru and 'anima' figures who emerged in his trance-like fantasies. This use of fantasy, which he later called 'active imagination', resembled the trance state induced by spiritualist mediums. For his doctoral dissertation at Basel University, Jung had attended and recorded the seances held by a young medium, his cousin Hélène Preiswerk. His mother's family, the Preiswerks, produced numerous ministers of religion, many with a keen interest in spiritualism and paranormal phenomena—an interest which Jung shared.

Two aspects of his cousin's performances during her seances particularly impressed Jung. One was how real her 'spirits' seemed to her: 'I see them before me', she told him, 'I can touch them, I speak to them about everything I wish as naturally as I'm talking to you. They must be real' (*CW* 1, para. 48). The other was the way in which a quite different, more dignified personality emerged when Hélène was in a trance. Her 'control' spirit, who said her name was 'Ivenes', spoke in perfect High German instead of Hélène's customary Basel dialect. Jung concluded that Ivenes was the mature, adult personality that was developing in Hélène's unconscious. The seances provided a means through which this development could proceed.

The origins of analytical psychology

In these observations we can detect the origins of two ideas which were to become central to the practice of analytical psychology: (1) that part-personalities or 'complexes' existing in the unconscious psyche can 'personate' in trances, dreams and hallucinations; and (2) that the real work of personality development proceeds at the unconscious level. These ideas, in turn, gave rise to (a) a therapeutic technique (*active imagination*) and (b) a teleological concept (*individuation*)—the notion that the goal of personal development is *wholeness*, to become as complete a human being as personal circumstances allow.

Jung's 'confrontation' with his own unconscious was conducted in the manner he had learned from Hélène Preiswerk. He wrote:

In order to seize hold of the fantasies, I frequently imagined a deep descent. I even made several attempts to get to the very bottom. The first time I reached, as it were, a depth of about a thousand feet; the next time I found myself at the edge of a cosmic abyss. It was like a voyage to the moon or a descent into an empty space. First came the image of a crater, and I had the feeling that I was in the land of the dead. The atmosphere was that of the other world. (*MDR*, p. 174).

Going down the steep descent was akin to entering a state of trance during which unconscious personalities emerged with sufficient clarity for him to hold conversations with them. Essentially, what he had discovered was a knack—the knack of descending into the underworld, like Odysseus, Heracles or Orpheus, while remaining fully conscious.

On one occasion he encountered an old man with a white beard, together with a beautiful young girl. They told him their names were Elijah and Salome and that they belonged together for all eternity. Jung came to understand these figures as the embodiment of two archetypes—the wise old man and the eternal feminine, and he identified them with the Logos and Eros principles. Soon, another personage arose out of the Elijah figure, and Jung called him Philemon.

Philemon appeared to him on numerous occasions and Jung declares that he learned many things from him, the most important being that there were events in his psyche that produced *themselves* as if they had a life of their own.

> In my fantasies I held conversations with him, and he said things which I had not consciously thought. For I observed clearly that it was he who spoke, not I. He said I treated thoughts as if I generated them myself, but in his view thoughts were like animals in the forest, or people in a room, or birds in the air, and added, "If you should see people in a room you would not think that you have made those people, or that you were responsible for them." (*MDR*, p. 176).

Like 'Ivenes' for Hélène, Philemon represented 'superior insight' for Jung. 'At times he seemed to me quite real, as if he were a living personality. I went walking up and down the garden with him, and he told me he was what the Indians call a guru' (*MDR*, p. 176). Like 'Ivenes' he was an 'attempt of the future personality to break through'.

It was also in the course of these fantasies that Jung first discovered the reality of what he was to call the 'anima' as an autonomous complex within himself. One day he asked himself, 'What am I really doing? Certainly it has nothing to do with science. But then what is it?' Whereupon he clearly heard a female voice within him say, 'It is art.' He was irritated by this interjection and replied emphatically, 'No, it is not art! On the contrary, it is nature' (*MDR*, p. 178). He resented the imputation that what he was doing was 'art' because if his unconscious emanations were contrived, then they were not the spontaneous productions of the 'natural mind' that he took them to be. He came to the conclusion that she must be the personification of his soul. In many traditions the soul is conceived of as feminine, and for this reason he gave her the Latin name 'anima'. 'I came to see that this inner feminine figure plays a typical, or archetypal, role in the unconscious of a man', and "anima" seemed the most appropriate name for her' (*MDR*, p. 174).

In one episode of active imagination Jung reported that a most disagreeable thing happened: 'Salome became very interested in me, and she assumed I could cure her blindness. She began to worship me. I said "Why do you worship me?" She replied, "You are Christ". In spite of my objections she maintained this. I said, "This is madness", and became filled with sceptical resistance.' (*Seminars*, vol. 3). In the course of this imaginary episode, Jung reported that a snake approached him, encircling and gripping his body. He assumed the attitude of the Crucifixion and felt that his face had taken on the aspect of a lion or a tiger. Years later, in a seminar with a select group of students, Jung amplified this experience in terms of Mithraic symbolism, identifying the lion-headed god gripped in the coils of a snake as Aion, *Deus Leontocephalus*, a statue of which exists in the Vatican Museum.

In his book *The Aryan Christ* (1997) Richard Noll attempted to argue that Jung was so crazy that he believed he had actually been 'deified' by this experience and become a god, the 'Aryan Christ', capable of saving the world. This interpretation is completely at variance with Jung's understanding of symbolic experience, and contrary to Jung's specific warnings to his patients and colleagues not to become identified with the powerful figures that can emerge during the course of active imagination. At times when unconscious events threatened to overwhelm him he understood how essential it was to keep a hold on reality. He would repeat to himself, 'I have a medical diploma from a Swiss university; I must help my patients; I have a wife and five children; I live at 228 Seestrasse in Küsnacht', in order to remind himself that he really existed and that he was not 'a blank page whirling about in the winds of the spirit, like Nietzsche', who went mad when he had similar experiences (*MDR*, pp. 181–82). What prevented these inner events from driving Jung mad was the creative attitude he adopted to them:

> I took great care to try to understand every single image, every item of my psychic inventory, and to classify them scientifically—so far as this was possible—and, above all, to realize them in actual life. That is what we usually neglect to do. We allow the images to rise up, and may be we wonder about them, but that is all. We do not take the trouble to understand them, let alone

draw ethical conclusions from them. (*MDR*, p. 184).

A culmination was reached soon after the Armistice in 1918 when Jung acted as commandant of a camp for British internees. A gifted amateur artist, his military duties being undemanding, he worked every morning on drawings in a notebook. These usually took the form of a 'mandala' (a Sanskrit term for a circular configuration incorporating the idea of quaternity and emphasizing the centre). He felt that these drawings enabled him to objectify and observe the transformations which his psyche was undergoing from day to day. He began to understand that the goal of all psychic development was realization of what he called the Self. He conceived this as the central nucleus of the entire personality. It contains the phylogenetic potential with which each of us is born, and the purpose of life is to actualize this potential in reality. To open oneself up to the dynamic resourcefulness of the Self is to transcend the petty concerns of the conscious ego and to enable intrapsychic healing to occur. This came to him with the force of a gnostic revelation: he *knew* it to be true. As a result, the stability that had eluded him for years came within his grasp: 'Gradually my inner peace returned' (*MDR*, p. 188).

Finally he had a dream in which he found himself in Liverpool (which literally means 'pool of life'). The various quarters of the city were arranged radially about a square (ie., in the form of a mandala):

> In the centre was a round pool, and in the middle of it a small island. While everything round about was obscured by rain, fog, smoke and dimly lit darkness, the little island blazed with sunlight. On it stood a single tree, a magnolia, in a shower of reddish blossoms. It was as though the tree stood in the sunlight and was at the same time the source of light. (*MDR*, p. 189).

This dream brought Jung a sense of finality. He felt that the unpleasant black of the fog represented what he had gone through up to that point. But now he had an image of great beauty with which he could go on living in the 'pool of life'. He experienced the whole episode as a profound process of personal transformation resulting in a radical shift in consciousness. Now he saw his way ahead. 'When I parted from Freud,' he wrote, 'I knew that I was plunging into the unknown. Beyond Freud, after all, I knew nothing; but I had taken the step into darkness. When that happens, and then such a dream comes, one feels it as an act of grace'

(*MDR*, p. 190).

Jungian Psychology as a 'subjective confession'

Freud remained bitter about Jung's 'defection' to the end of his life, accusing Jung of 'cowardice' in the face of the facts of sexuality. Yet of the two, Freud was the sexually frustrated one. As Paul Roazen has said, 'Jung may have rejected Freud's concepts of sexuality, but then he had less personal need to make sex seem all-important.' For years members of the 'Freud Squad' continued to level accusations of 'cowardice', 'resistance', and 'flight from the unconscious' at all those whom they convicted of betraying orthodox Freudian ideology. It was the sort of charge that Melanie Klein was later to repeat against John Bowlby. Such attacks were made with a humourless, carping insistence, which revealed a remarkable lack of psychological insight and an incredible capacity for unconscious projection. Freud never considered that he may have done harm to others, but was intensely aware of the wrongs other people had done to him. As he wrote in 1915, 'I have never done anything shameful or malicious, nor do I find in myself any temptation to do so ... others are brutal and unreliable ...' (Roazen, 1992, p. 262). When, on one occasion, Jung mildly commented how ambitious Freud was, Freud said, 'Me? I'm the most humble of men and the only man who isn't ambitious.' With wry wit, Jung replied, 'That's a big thing—to be the only one!'

On recovery from their creative illnesses, both Freud and Jung published major works: Freud's: *The Interpretation of Dreams* in 1899 and Jung's *Psychological Types* in 1921. In *Psychological Types* Jung began to organize his ideas about the structure and function of the psyche and to examine the basis of his differences with Freud. From a wide-ranging review of cultural history he concluded that two fundamental psychological orientations are apparent, which he called *introverted* and *extraverted attitudes*. Introversion is characterized by an inward movement of interest away from the outer world to the inner world of the subject; extraversion, by an outward movement of interest away from the subject to the outer realm of objective reality. This distinction between introverted and extraverted attitude types has found wide acceptance, even among academic psychologists hostile to analysis, like Hans Eysenck.

Jung recognized that every psychological system, whether that devised by Freud, by Adler, or by himself, grew out of the psychology of its originator: it was in the nature of a subjective confession. 'Even when I am dealing with empirical data', he wrote, 'I am necessarily speaking about myself' (*CW* 4, para. 774). In advanced old age, he added: 'My life is what I have done, my scientific work; the one is inseparable from the other. The work is an expression of my inner development' (*MDR*, p. 211). What had drawn him into psychiatry in the first place was the idea, expressed in Krafft-Ebing's *Textbook of Psychiatry*, that mental illnesses were 'diseases of the personality' and that to treat them meant that the psychiatrist must engage them with his whole personality. Inevitably, Jung's enthusiasm for this idea engendered a personal approach to the analytic relationship which was much warmer, more intimate and emotionally committed than that advocated by Freud.

The transpersonal perspective

Because of his introverted concern with subjective experiences such as he had encountered in his 'confrontation with the unconscious', Jung's approach to psychology has been generally discounted as 'less scientific' than Freud's. This is doubly unfair: not only have Freud's scientific credentials been seriously impugned, but Jung is seldom given adequate acknowledgement for his attempt to ground his own concepts in biology. By adopting a transpersonal perspective, Jung sought to examine the life of the individual, not only in the context of his or her culture, but in the context of human existence as a whole. 'Ultimately', he wrote, 'every individual life is at the same time the eternal life of the species' (*CW* 11, para. 146).

As a consequence, Jung's model of the psyche is imbued with biological assumptions. Not only did he consider the archetypal structure of the collective unconscious to have an evolutionary origin but he maintained that the psyche functioned in accordance with the biological principles of adaptation, homeostasis and epigenesis. Thus, in Jung's view, the human infant, far from being a *tabula rasa*, is a highly complex creature, endowed with a huge repertoire of built-in expectations, demands and patterns of response, whose fulfilment depends on appropriate stimuli arising in the environment.

The sum total of this endowment, as we have already seen, Jung called the Self, which he often referred to as 'the archetype of archetypes'. The other psychic structures that he described—the ego, persona, shadow, animus or anima—all develop out of this matrix and remain under the guiding influence of the Self. The goal of the Self is wholeness, and it is this lifelong quest that Jung called *individuation*—the attainment of the fullest possible self-realization in the psyche and in the world. In religious terms this is symbolized by the incarnation of God in the human form of Christ.

Though Jung felt the anima (the contrasexual complex in the male) to be identified with the soul, it, like the animus in the female, is at the same time part of an evolved system responsible for initiating and maintaining the heterosexual bond. Seen in this light, both animus and anima are indispensable to the survival of the species. Together they represent a supreme pair of opposites, the *syzygy*, 'giving the promise of union and actually making it possible'.

That the psyche is an efficient organ of adaptation is because it evolved in the context of the world. The laws which prevail in the cosmos also prevail in the psyche because the psyche is, in his words, 'pure nature'. For this reason, Jung referred to the collective unconscious as the *objective psyche*, because it is as real and as existent as anything in nature. This explains why fundamental natural laws, like the principles of adaptation, homeostasis and growth, apply to the psyche just as surely as to any other biological phenomenon.

Homeostasis is the principle of self-regulation. It is the means by which biological systems keep themselves in a state of balance in the interests of survival. Natural environments on our planet are constantly changing, and no living organisms could have evolved had they not possessed within themselves the capacity to maintain a steady state. Accordingly, Jung viewed the psyche, like the body, as a self-regulating system, which strives perpetually to maintain a balance between opposing propensities, while, at the same time, actively seeking its own individuation. Just as the body possesses control mechanisms to keep its vital functions in balance, so the psyche has a control mechanism in the compensatory activity of dreams.

The significance of dreams

Here again, it is true to say that Jung's approach to the psychology of dreaming was more compatible with biological thinking than Freud's. He viewed the function of dreams as being to promote better adaptation to life by compensating the one-sided limitations of the dreamer's conscious attitudes, and he rejected Freud's idea that the dream is a facade concealing its true meaning: the so-called facade of most houses is by no means a fake or a deceptive distortion; on the contrary, it follows the plan of the building and often betrays the interior arrangement' (*CW* 7, para. 319). In other words, 'dreams are the direct expression of unconscious psychic activity' (*CW* 7, para. 295). They provide a view of the dreamer's situation and mobilize the potential of the personality to meet it. The compensatory function of dreams is derived from the rich capacity of the unconscious to create symbols, to think laterally, and to derive information from a pool of data far more extensive than that directly available to consciousness.

One of the most eminent of modern dream researchers, J. Allan Hobson of Harvard University came round to a position very close to Jung's: 'I differ from Freud in that I think that most dreams are neither obscure nor bowdlerized, but rather that they are transparent and unedited', Hobson declared, 'They reveal clearly meaningful, undisguised and often highly conflictual themes worthy of note by the dreamer (and any interpretive assistant). My position echoes Jung's notion of dreams as transparently meaningful and does away with any distinction between manifest and latent content' (1988, p. 12).

As an efficient adaptive, homeostatic system, the psyche, in Jung's view, possessed the capacity to heal itself, and it was in the compensatory function of the unconscious that this power for self-healing resided. For him, a vital expression of this propensity was the way in which the unconscious gave rise to symbols capable of reuniting conflicting tendencies that seemed irreconcilable at the conscious level. Jung called this phenomenon the *transcendent function*. He argued that we are never able to solve the most crucial problems in life, but we can, if we are patient, transcend them. Describing this, Jung wrote:

Here and there it happened in my practice that a patient grew beyond the dark possibilities within himself, and the observation of the fact was an experience of foremost importance to me. In the meantime, I had learned to see that the greatest and most important problems of life were all fundamentally insoluble. They must be so, because they express the necessary polarity inherent in every self-regulating system. They can never be solved, but only outgrown. (1962, p. 91).

Growth, development, individuation, Self-realization, these are the themes to which Jung returned again and again. He saw the whole life-cycle as a continuing process of metamorphosis which was regulated by the Self. Conducting us through the life cycle, the Self causes us to re-create images, ideas, symbols and emotions similar to those that human beings have always experienced since our species began and wherever on this planet we have taken up our abode. As the life cycle unfolds, so we accept and incorporate into our personalities our personal experience of living. But we are aware only of our personal history; we are unconscious of the evolutionary blueprint on whose basis our personal experience proceeds. This helps to explain how it is that some of the best minds of the twentieth century have rejected an evolutionary approach to human nature in favour of behaviourist theories that looked no further than the conditioning to which each individual is subjected in his or her own lifetime. By ignoring the archetypal dimension, they neglected the biological bedrock on which each human personality is built. But there are signs that at last this is beginning to change.

The archetypes of the collective unconscious

Of all Jung's ideas, none has proved more controversial than his theory of a collective unconscious. Yet it is a hypothesis which has been rediscovered and reproposed by specialists in a number of different disciplines. Jung used it to explain the existence in humans of certain psychic and behavioural characteristics which, while achieving unique expression in each individual are, at the same time, universally present in all members of our species. 'I have chosen the term "collective" because this part of the unconscious is not individual but universal; in contrast to the personal psyche, it has contents and modes of behaviour that are more or less the same everywhere and in all individuals' (*CW* 9i, para. 3). Jung related this 'common psychic substrate of a suprapersonal nature' to the structure of the brain:

Every man is born with a brain that is profoundly differentiated, and this

94

makes him capable of very various mental functions, which are neither onto-genetically developed or acquired ... This particular circumstance explains, for example, the remarkable analogies presented by the unconscious in the most remotely separated races and peoples.

It is apparent, he says, in the extraordinary correspondence that exists between the myths, folk tales, religious beliefs and rituals that occur throughout the world.

The universal similarity of human brains leads us then to admit the existence of a certain psychic function, identical with itself in all individuals; we call it the collective psyche. (*CW* 9i, paras. 453–54).

This is such a reasonable position to adopt that it is a puzzle to under-stand why Jung's proposal encountered as much opposition as it did. A major difficulty was that it subverted the prevailing academic consensus (what has been called the Standard Social Science Model or SSSM), which eschewed biological thinking altogether and was deeply hostile to the idea that innate structures could have any part to play in human psy-chology or human social behaviour. In many quarters the SSSM still pre-vails, though there are signs that its global influence is beginning to wane, together with its principle article of faith that in human affairs 'cultural evolution has replaced biological evolution'.

Another difficulty arose from Jung's terminology. For many, the term 'collective unconscious' had an unmistakably mystical ring to it, as if Jung believed in the existence of a 'group mind' or 'world soul'. Initial-ly, he also used the term 'primordial image' for what he was later to call an 'archetype', and this suggested a Lamarckian belief in the inheritance of intact and pre-formed innate images—a notion quite unacceptable to biologists. Jung later corrected this error by making a clear distinction between the archetype-as-such and the ideas, images and behaviour pat-terns that the archetype-as-such gave rise to.

Though he remained all his life primarily interested in the psychic as-pects of archetypes, he nevertheless understood that a strictly scientific approach would make more headway if it concentrated on their behav-ioural manifestations. As he himself insisted, the archetype 'is not meant to denote an inherited idea, but rather an inherited mode of functioning, corresponding to the inborn way in which the chick emerges from the egg, the bird builds its nest, a certain kind of wasp stings the motor ganglion of the caterpillar and eels find their way to the Bermudas. In other words, it is a "pattern of behaviour". *This aspect of the archetype, the purely biological one, is the proper concern of scientific psychology'* (*CW* 18, para.1228; italics added).

In my *Archetype: A Natural History of the Self* (Stevens, 1982), I drew attention to the many striking parallels which exist between the concepts of analytical psychology and those of ethology (the branch of behavioural science that studies animals in their natural habitats) and suggested a fruitful interaction between the two disciplines would become more feasible if Jung's terminology were modified: I proposed the term *phylogenetic psyche* to replace 'collective unconscious' and *innate neuropsychic units* or *potentials* to replace 'archetypes'. I went on to argue that, if Jungians wish to place analytical psychology on a sound scientific basis, they would do well to draw closer to the ethologists and become aware of the discoveries which were being made not only in the observation of animal behaviour but in the cross-cultural studies of human communities throughout the world. Since then, a number of evolutionary psychologists and psychiatrists on both sides of the Atlantic have detected and announced the presence of neuropsychic propensities which are virtually indistinguishable from archetypes. These have been variously termed 'response patterns', 'master programs', 'propensity states', 'response strategies', 'evolved psychological mechanisms' and 'modules': all are held responsible for the crucial, species-specific patterns of behaviour and psychological functions that evolved because they maximized the fitness of the organism to survive, and for its genes to survive, in the environment in which it evolved. These strategies are inherently shared by all members of the species, whether they be healthy or ill.

The significance of these developments for all psychotherapeutic disciplines cannot be overemphasized, and I shall return to them in Volume 3. They provide the theoretical basis for a science of human development and for a systematic approach to human psychology. Psychopathology can then be understood to occur when 'archetypal' strategies malfunction as a result of environmental insults or deficiencies at critical stages of development. A sound theoretical basis in terms of which hypotheses can be formulated will enable these insults and deficiencies to be empirically investigated and defined. Though Jung is seldom mentioned by evolutionary psychologists, his primacy in introducing the archetypal hypothesis into psychology must be acknowledged: it was one of the truly seminal ideas of the twentieth century.

Jungian therapy in theory and practice

Another area in which Jung has not been given his due is his contribution to the actual practice of psychotherapy. The innovations he introduced have had an influence which extends far beyond his own school, and it is fair to say that this influence has been benevolent and humane. Though his initial formulations arose mainly out of his own creative illness, they were also a conscious reaction against the stereotype of the classical Freudian analyst, sitting silent and aloof behind the couch, occasionally emitting *ex cathedra* pronouncements and interpretations, while remaining totally uninvolved in the patient's guilt, anguish, and need for reassurance and support. Instead, Jung offered the radical proposal that analysis is a dialectical procedure, a two-way exchange between two people, who are equally involved. Although this was a revolutionary idea when he first suggested it, it is a model that has influenced psychotherapists of most schools, though many seem not to realize that it originated with Jung.

Jung's attitude to patients, his approach to mental illness, the principles and techniques he advocated in treatment, and his views on the role of the therapist were all radically different from those of Freud. In place of Freud's surgical detachment, Jung advocated a warmer, more welcoming atmosphere in the consulting room. Many people who consulted him have testified to the cordiality with which they were received. His sense of humour was always in evidence and he made no secret of his own vulnerabilities and shortcomings. For example, one deeply worried woman was immediately reassured when he greeted her with a grin and said, 'So you're in the soup, too!' He believed patients should be treated with the same courtesy that one would extend to any respected visitor and that every appointment should be regarded as a social occasion as well as a clinical interview. Accordingly, he never used a couch or any obvious techniques or tricks of the trade, treating people as essentially normal and healthy, while giving serious attention to any problems they might bring. 'If the person has a neurosis', he told his London colleague E. A. Bennet, 'that is something extra, but people should be regarded as normal and met socially' (Bennet, 1982).

My own analyst, Irene Champernowne, who was herself analysed by Jung, told me that what struck her most was the extent to which he committed his whole attention to the material that emerged in the analytic hour: he was completely there, she said, not aloof and out of sight, not a screen for projections, not a transference manipulator, but there as a real person. What was more, he gave you the feeling that he was working with you not just because he was your analyst but because, through you, he was pursuing his own research, and was learning from the process. This gave a sense of heightened importance to the proceedings. Jung confirmed this in his autobiography:

> My patients brought me so close to the reality of human life that I could not help learning essential things from them. Encounters with people of so many different kinds and on so many different psychological levels have been for me incomparably more important than fragmentary conversations with celebrities. (*MDR*, p. 143).

Unlike Freud, Jung did his best to eschew dogma. When E. A. Bennet told him in 1951 that he was writing an article about him for *The British Medical Journal,* Jung said at once: 'Whatever you say, make it clear that I have no dogma, I'm still open and haven't got things fixed.' His advice to Irene Champernowne and to all his students was, 'Learn your theories, and then, when the patient walks in through the door, forget them.'

Symptom formation as a creative act

In evolving his approach to mental illness, Jung was reacting not only against the concepts of Freudian psychoanalysis but also against the ideas that prevailed, and to a large extent still prevail, in conventional psychiatry. The traditional pathological approach describes mental illnesses as distinct entities, each presenting a clearly defined clinical picture. Jung considered this to be rewarding up to a point, but saw that it had the disadvantage of thrusting all the inessential features of the condition to 'the forefront, while covering up the one aspect that is essential, and that is the patient's intensely personal and individual story:

'To my mind, therapy only really begins after the investigation of that wholly personal story. It is the patient's secret, the rock against which he is shattered. If I know his secret story, I have a key to the treatment ... In therapy the problem is always the whole person, never the symptom alone. We must ask questions which challenge the whole personality' (*MDR*, p. 118). 'Clinical diagnoses are important,' he acknowledged, 'since they give the doctor a certain orientation. But they do not help the patient' (*MDR*, p. 124).

Behind all psychiatric symptomatology, even the most bizarrely psychotic, we find age-old human conflicts: 'At bottom we discover nothing new and unknown in the mentally ill, rather we encounter the substratum of our own natures' (*MDR*, p. 127). In Jung's view, psychiatric symptoms were persistent exaggerations of natural psychophysiological responses, and this view has been reaffirmed by contemporary psychiatrists who use ethological concepts in their approach to mental illness. For example, Dr Brant Wenegrat of the Stanford University Medical Center in California has argued that all psychopathological syndromes, whether psychotic, neurotic or psychopathic, are statistically abnormal manifestations of 'innate response strategies' (his term for archetypes) shared by all individuals whether they are mentally healthy or ill.

Jung carried this insight one very important stage further, arguing that symptom formation is itself a product of the individuation process, that illness is, in other words, a creative act, a function of the psyche's imperative to grow and develop even in abnormal circumstances. Neurosis is thus to be conceived as a form of adaptation—albeit an inferior adaptation—of a potentially healthy organism responding to the demands of life. Because certain archetypal needs essential to the program of development have not been met at the appropriate time in the patient's past, he or she experiences difficulty in achieving a mature adjustment and, as a consequence, individuation follows a course into illness rather than healthy self-completion.

An important distinction has to be made here between Jung's and Freud's approaches to the causes of neurosis. Unlike Freud, Jung did not hold that the origins of a neurosis invariably lie in early childhood. On the contrary, Jung maintained that neurosis is caused by a failure to meet the contemporary challenges of life. Neurosis may occur at any stage of the life cycle as a response to outer events, such as going to a new school, losing a parent or spouse, starting a new job, being conscripted into the Army, getting married or divorced, bearing one's first child, and so on. Earlier traumata may predispose an individual to exhibit neurotic symptoms, it is true, but such traumas are not the cause of the neurosis. Neurosis is, therefore, in Jung's view, essentially an escape from a challenging life event that the individual feels unequipped to meet. Consequently, Jung taught his students, when confronted with a new patient, to ask themselves, 'What task is this patient trying to avoid?'

A fair proportion of Jung's patients had little that was psychiatrically wrong with them. This is in accord with contemporary findings that 30–50 per cent of patients seeking psychotherapy do not meet the criteria of any disorder (Westen et al., 2004) 'About a third of my cases', wrote Jung, 'are not suffering from any clearly definable neurosis, but from the senselessness and aimlessness of their lives. I should not object if there were called the general neurosis of our age' (*CW* 16, para. 83). To what did he attribute this 'general neurosis'? He put it down to a collective 'loss of soul': to a loss of contact with the great mythic and religious symbols of our culture, and to the emergence of social institutions which alienate us from our archetypal nature.

Jung argued that the more secular, materialistic and compulsively extraverted our civilization became, the greater the unhappiness, 'senselessness and aimlessness' of our lives. What was the answer? Not a return to the church since his own experience had taught him that organized religion meant spiritual death. Again as a result of his own experience, he felt that we have no other recourse than to abandon the exclusively extraverted quest for meaning in the outer world of material objects and, instead, establish contact with the symbol-forming capacities latent within our own psychic nature. What was needed was hard psychological work to open our minds to the inner wealth of the unconscious in order to realize in actuality our own capacity for wholeness. In the process, he believed that meaning and purpose would flood back into our lives, as it had into his own:

> I have frequently seen people become neurotic when they content themselves with inadequate or wrong answers to life. They seek position, marriage, reputation, outward success or money, and remain unhappy and

neurotic even when they have attained what they were seeking. Such people are usually confined within too narrow a spiritual horizon. Their life has not sufficient content, sufficient meaning. If they are enabled to develop into more spacious personalities, the neurosis generally disappears. For that reason the idea of development was always of the highest importance to me.

One important virtue of conceiving symptom formation as a creative act is that it gives rise to therapeutic optimism. Instead of regarding symptoms as futile forms of suffering, they can be understood as the growing pains of a soul struggling to escape fear and find fulfilment. Neurosis, said Jung, in the nearest he came to a definition, is the suffering of a soul that has not found its meaning.

Analysis and synthesis: therapeutic alchemy

If you present yourself for Jungian analysis, what are you letting yourself in for? As a rough guide, Jung divided analysis broadly into four stages, which inevitably overlap and certainly do not always proceed in a regular order. These are *confession, elucidation, education* and *transformation.*

Confession is the stage when one shares one's story with the analyst, offering up one's guilty secrets and feelings of self-doubt and personal inadequacy. This is cathartic in that one feels one has shed a burden or discharged a load of poison. One begins to feel less isolated with one's problems and, in Jung's terminology, the integration of the shadow begins (that is, one starts to acknowledge in consciousness the inferior parts of oneself that have been kept hidden not only from everyone else but from oneself.

Elucidation is roughly akin to Freudian interpretive analysis in that symptoms and transference phenomena are examined, not with a single-minded search for sexual traumata (though these may, of course, emerge), but with a view to detecting areas of failed development or what I have called 'the frustration of archetypal intent' (Stevens, 1982).

In the educative phase, the insights gained in the first two stages are 'amplified' by examining parallels in myth, folk tale, art and literature, so as to establish the cultural and archetypal contexts of one's personal mythology or, as Adler called it, the 'guiding fiction' which has ruled one's life. One thus begins to experience oneself as a member of the human species, a living part of its history; and this usually goes along with an improved adaptation to the demands of society.

Transformation occurs through one's own 'confrontation with the unconscious': one comes face-to-face with the part-personalities active in one's unconscious psyche. These function in a naturally homeostatic manner in order to compensate for one's previously narrow, neurotic or one-sided development. By this stage, a lot of homework becomes necessary outside the analytic situation, recording one's dreams, working up associations to them, making some representation of their imagery (drawing or painting them or modelling them in clay), amplifying their symbolism by consulting the literature; doing active imagination, and so on. At this stage, the 'transcendent function' of symbols comes into its own, and, provided one can accept full ethical responsibility for what is released from the unconscious, the individuation process is well under way. It is accompanied by a growing sense of 'selfhood', a state reaching beyond mere 'normality' or 'social adaptation' to a full affirmation and acceptance of oneself as a whole entity in one's own right.

To elucidate the analytical process itself, Jung drew analogies from alchemy. Not surprisingly, this was treated with scepticism, often amounting to frank incredulity, especially among academic psychologists and those who liked to see themselves as hard-headed, 'scientific' psychoanalysts. Jung's interest in alchemy arose from his insight that this primordial science could be understood as an imaginative form of 'projective identification' with the transformative processes occurring in matter.

Having little or no objective knowledge of these processes, alchemists projected their fantasies about them into what they were observing, and in so doing were unconsciously revealing those very processes as they occurred in themselves. Alchemy and astrology were of interest to Jung, not because he believed that it was possible to turn base objects into gold or read one's personal destiny in the stars, but because they represented repositories of generations of human psychological investment. They were artefacts produced by the activity of the objective psyche. By studying these projections, he believed he could gain valuable insight into the archetypal structures at the core of psychic experience and functioning.

Though he liked to think that he proceeded in an orderly and scientific manner in collecting material to amplify his concept of a collective unconscious, Jung acknowledged that analysis, like alchemy, is not a science but an art, an *ars spagyrica*. 'Spagyric' is derived from two Greek words, *span* meaning to stretch out (i.e., to analyse) and *ageirein*, to collect together (i.e., to synthesize). The alchemical slogan *solve et coagula* (dissolve and coagulate) precisely expresses these two steps: 'The alchemist saw the essence of his art in separation and analysis on the one hand and synthesis and consolidation on the other' (Foreword to *CW* 14). The analytic phase corresponds to the reductive method of Freud and the first two stages of Jungian analysis, and the synthetic phase, to the last two stages.

Whether or not an analysis succeeds in its objectives depends on the raw materials (the alchemical *prima materia*) which patient and analyst bring with them to the analytic situation (the alchemical retort, the *vas*) and the transformation that occurs through their interaction. The first requirement is that both accept full responsibility for themselves and their own contribution to the relationship: 'The doctor must emerge from his anonymity and give an account of himself, just as he expects his patients to do' (*CW* 16, para. 23). Initially, many patients find it hard to accept responsibility for themselves and for their problems, preferring to hold others responsible and to adopt a passive or dependent attitude to the analyst. But this has to change if the analysis is ever to progress beyond the second stage: 'The real therapy only begins when the patient sees that it is no longer father and mother who are standing in his way, but himself …' (*CW* 7, para. 88).

The techniques of classical Jungian analysis—the two chairs, the dialectical mutuality between analyst and patient, the practice of instituting relatively frequent breaks in the analysis and a progressive reduction in the number of sessions, the personal work on dreams and 'active imagination' outside the analytic situation—are all designed to heighten a sense of responsibility in the patient for his or her own process of growth. Jung banished the couch from the consulting room because he found it made the patient passive and dependent on the analyst, and positively encouraged a Freudian regression to the infantile complexes. This inevitably hindered the onset of the collaborative, prospective adventure that Jung conceived analysis to be. Although he took full account of the patient's experience of the past, he was far more interested in what the patient was in the process of becoming in the present and the future. Sitting face-to-face on similar chairs also made it easier for both therapist and patient to experience themselves as colleagues working on a shared task and to test the reality of whatever transference or countertransference projections they might make on one another.

Interestingly in the light of recent research which would tend to support Jung's view, he was critical of the Freudian practice of seeing patients intensively over long periods of time:

> The psychoanalyst thinks he must see his patients for an hour a day for months on end; I manage in difficult cases with three or four sittings a week. As a rule I content myself with two, and once the patient has got going, he is reduced to one. In the interim he has to work on himself, but under my control. I provide him with the necessary psychological knowledge to free himself from my medical authority as speedily as possible. In addition, I break off the treatment every ten weeks or so, in order to throw him back on his normal milieu ... In such a procedure time can take effect as a healing factor, without the patient's having to pay for the doctor's time. With proper direction most people become capable after a while of making their contribution—however modest at first—to the common work. In my experience the absolute period of cure is not shortened by too many sittings. (*CW* 16, para. 43).

Contemporary research leads to similar conclusions. Yet many analytic organizations continue to insist that patients must attend at least three or four times a week over long periods of time; otherwise, they insist, the patient is not getting proper analysis and therefore not receiving adequate treatment. Unless these organizations can produce evidence in support of this contention, they should face up to a need to reconsider their position.

Analysing to live

One aspect of Jung's practice which most analysts have chosen to ignore (often for financial reasons) is his advice to break off the analysis every ten weeks to throw the patient back into life, to discourage dependence on the analyst, and to encourage reliance on the Self. Then the patient does not live to analyse, but analyses to live. This can be of immense benefit to analysts as well as to patients, for it helps prevent the exhaustion that can so easily afflict hard-working therapists and ensure against their work becoming routine or lifeless. Provided they can afford it, a regular break from clinical responsibilities can enable analysts to follow other pursuits, such as studying, writing, lecturing, painting, pottery, travel, sport and participating more fully in the lives of their family and friends, so that they can recharge their creative energies and strengthen their immunity to those forms of psychic contagion and 'burn out' that are common among therapists, social workers and psychiatrists. Jung could afford to do this because he married a rich wife. Others are less fortunately placed, but it remains an ideal goal.

However, a number of patients find it impossible to work in the manner that Jung advocated, especially those who, as a result of defective parenting in childhood, suffer from personality disorders or from what Bowlby called 'anxious attachment'. Such patients need time to establish with their analyst a working relationship through which they can begin to conceive of themselves as capable of sustaining a lasting bond of intimacy and trust. Only when this has been achieved can they benefit from the kind of imaginative work with the unconscious that Jung regarded as the crux of analysis. Apart from these and some other exceptions, the classical Jungian approach seems to be of help to patients with widely differing kinds of personal difficulties and neurotic disorders, although a great deal of research needs to be done to substantiate this. In Jung's view, the factor of primary importance determining the success or failure of treatment is the personality of the analyst. For this reason Jung introduced the training analysis as an indispensable requirement for becoming an analyst, while he was still a member of Freud's psychoanalytic circle. 'You must yourself be the real stuff,' he wrote. 'If you are not, God help you! Then you will lead your patients astray. Therefore you must first accept an analysis of yourself' (*MDR*, p. 134). Elsewhere he wrote: 'An ancient adept has said: "If the wrong man uses the right means, the right means work in the wrong way." This Chinese saying, unfortunately, only too true, stands in sharp contrast to our belief in the "right" method irrespective of the man who applies it. In reality, everything depends on the man and little or nothing on the method' (*CW* 13, para. 4).

Once again, Jung's opinion is in line with recent research which has established that the personal qualities of the analyst and the quality of the relationship he or she succeeds in forming with the patient contribute more reliably to a positive outcome than the theoretical orientation or the professional qualification of the analyst.

Not only is it necessary, in Jung's opinion, for analysts to be analysed during their training, but they must continue to work on themselves throughout their professional life. The analyst must go on learning endlessly, he wrote, for only what he can put right in himself can he hope to put right in the patient. Continuing self-analysis is necessary because of Jung's conception of what the analytic relationship entails, namely a commitment on the part of the analyst that is at least as great as that of the patient. At the unconscious level both doctor and patient are participating in what the alchemists termed a *coniunctio*: like two chemical substances, they are drawn together in the analytic situation by affinity, and their interaction produces change: 'When two chemical substances combine, both are altered. This is precisely what happens in the transference' (*CW* 16, para. 358).

An archetypal relationship

Jung greatly extended the Freudian view of the transference. He understood that the healer–patient relationship is an archetypal relationship which has been with us since the beginning of time. In the course of an analysis, archetypal images are stirred up which, when projected onto the person of the analyst, can confer upon him or her great therapeutic (or destructive) power. In Jung's own experience, such numinous figures as the magician, shaman, witch-doctor, guru, priest and wise old man were commonly projected.

Most importantly from the point of view of therapeutic outcome, the analyst can receive the projection of previously unfulfilled archetypal needs. For example, he may become the powerful father figure that a patient lacked in childhood, and this was clearly a crucial component of Jung's own transference onto the person of Freud. Finally, unconscious activity in the patient causes reciprocal activity in the unconscious of the analyst, with the result that the bond between them is transformed into something much more profound than the conventional doctor–patient relationship. It is this aspect of the transference that makes it essential that the therapist should be thoroughly analysed and made aware of what

Jung called his 'personal equation'. It then becomes possible for the analyst to recognize what is unconsciously projected onto the patient (the so-called *countertransference*) and to use this constructively in the therapeutic relationship, instead of allowing it to become disruptive.

Moreover, in contrast to analysts of other schools, Jung laid stress on the vital importance of *feeling* as an indispensable catalyst influencing all transactions between analyst and patient. Jung pointed out that feeling also has to be present in the ego's relationship with the unconscious no less than in the analytic relationship itself. This is particularly true when patient and analyst are both of the same sex, success depending on each being in a feeling relationship with the other's unconscious and the material arising from it. Some over-rational patients try to understand 'with their brains only', observed Jung. 'And when they have understood, they think they have done their full share of realization. That they should also have a feeling relationship to the contents of the unconscious seems strange to them or even ridiculous' (*CW* 16, para. 489). Yet unless feeling is present, the prospects for growth and transformation are not good.

Jung's assertion that the personalities of both analyst and patient must be fully committed in a feeling relationship if the analysis is to succeed is contrary to the teaching of both Freudian and Kleinian schools but entirely compatible with recent studies of the essential factors contributing to positive therapeutic outcome. Freudians and Kleinians have always criticized Jung for lacking their scientific objectivity, for abandoning Freud's deterministic and mechanistic outlook, and for rejecting the coherent explanatory system that they believed Freud had developed from a set of strictly scientific propositions. In the light of highly critical reviews of the Freudian literature and current studies of psychotherapeutic effectiveness, we are now in a position to form a more balanced opinion concerning the appropriateness of Jung's views.

Where Jung still leaves many people unconvinced and bewildered, however, is when he goes beyond science to eschew the laws of cause and effect, to embrace a universe in which 'synchronistic' events can transcend the barriers of space and time, as in the phenomena of telepathy, clairvoyance, extrasensory perception, reincarnation, spiritualism and communication with the dead. For one of his background and upbringing, it is not surprising that he should always have been interested in such phenomena and more than half-inclined to believe in their actuality. The fact that current scientific laws could not account for them was no reason, in his view, for not giving them due consideration or for declining to propose possible hypotheses to account for them. These ideas, which had preoccupied him as a student when he lectured about them at his University Zofingia Society, returned to haunt him as he approached old age. He sought to penetrate what he perceived to be the unitary reality which underlay all manifest phenomena—the *unus mundus* of mystical tradition, the 'eternal ground of all being'. Having conceived the archetypes as possessing a fundamental duality, having both a psychic and a neurological structure (the two poles of 'spirit' and 'matter'), he now began to see archetypes as mediators of the *unus mundus*, responsible for organizing not merely ideas and images in the psyche but the fundamental principles of matter and energy in the physical world as well.

In advancing this proposition, Jung attracted no less a person than the Nobel Physics Laureate Wolfgang Pauli, who argued that by conceiving archetypes in this way Jung had discovered the 'missing link' between the physical events (which are the legitimate study of science) and the mind of the scientist who studies them. In other words, the archetypes which order our perceptions and ideas are themselves the product of an objective order which transcends both the human mind and the external world. At this supreme point physical science, psychology and theology all coalesce.

It is hard to escape the conclusion that the alienation between Freud and Jung was a personal misfortune for them both and an historical misfortune for psychoanalysis. Their bitter division drove both men hard in opposite directions, taking their followers with them. It made Freud reaffirm his dedication to the principles of causality and psychic determinism, causing him to concentrate on the psychopathology of childhood and to reject religion as an infantile desire for parental protection. Jung countered by adopting a teleological perspective: he endorsed the freedom of the will, extended the developmental process beyond childhood to the whole span of life, proposed that psychiatric symptoms were themselves an attempt at adaptation, and saw the spiritual life as the fulfilment of a basic human need. Freud persisted in the view that symbolism was essentially the product of pathological, defensive processes; while Jung conceived it as a natural function of the psyche's quest for meaning, balance and self-completion, and as an expression of the self-correcting and self-healing capacities inherent in human nature. To Freud the unconscious was and remained a Zuider Zee of repressed infantile urges to be drained in the service of the ego; to Jung it was an inexhaustible source of life-enriching potential. Where Freud conceived civilization as a consequence of the necessary repression and sublimation of atavistic urges, Jung developed the view that Western society was compounding the mistake of the alchemists, projecting its spiritual aspirations into material things in the delusion that it was pursuing the highest goal.

So it was that, in Jung, psychoanalysis lost a priceless asset. His continued adherence could have transformed the course of its development, giving it a profounder, broader, more imaginative view of the human psyche. Instead, psychoanalysis was to continue to trudge along the reductive path on which Freud had set it, persisting in an obsessive preoccupation with the real and imagined experiences of infancy, getting locked in conjectural disputes about their supposed significance; while virtually ignoring the formative influences of events occurring throughout the rest of life.

As the century wore on, some psychoanalysts were to move covertly in the Jungian direction (denying that they were doing so), while some Jungians, like Michael Fordham in England, moved openly in the Freudian direction. As the historian of psychoanalysis, Paul Roazen, has commented, 'Few responsible figures in psychoanalysis would be disturbed today if an analyst were to present views identical to Jung's in 1913.' Such are the ironies of history. However, it is my belief that a true rapprochement will not be achieved between these contrasting traditions until their differences are transcended through the adoption of a new paradigm taking full account of the phylogeny, the evolutionary background, the natural history of the Self.

GLOSSARY

Abreaction: the discharge of emotion associated with disturbing experiences suffered in the past; advocated by Joseph Breuer and Sigmund Freud as the most effective treatment for hysteria. Their claims for the success of the method have subsequently proved to be exaggerated. Abreaction is still used, however, albeit in modified form, in the treatment of post-traumatic stress disorder.

Aetiology: that part of medical science that investigates the causes of disease.

Algorithm: a genetically acquired learning mechanism that organizes experience into adaptive patterns specific to certain typical activities, such as mate selection, predator avoidance, site selection, and so on.

Amplification: a technique advocated by Jung for working with symbolic material (arising from dreams, fantasies, paintings, etc.). Whereas free association may reveal much about the personal context of a dream, amplification educes parallels from myth, literature, art, religion and anthropology to 'make ample' the symbolism involved and extend its range of meaning to the human condition as a whole.

Analytical psychologist: an analyst who subscribes to the theories and who practises the therapeutic approach advocated by C. G. Jung; to be distinguished from psychiatrist, psychoanalyst, psychologist and psychotherapist.

Archetypes: a term introduced by C. G. Jung to denote innate neuropsychic centres possessing the capacity to initiate, control and mediate the common behavioural characteristics and typical experiences of all human beings irrespective of race, culture, creed or historical epoch. In the Jungian scheme of things, archetypes are the components of the collective unconscious

Behaviourism: a theoretical approach to animal and human psychology that focuses on the objective study of actual behavioural responses while largely ignoring the existence of feelings or states of mind, since these are not public and not objectively verifiable.

Biosocial goals: the social goals for which we are biologically equipped to strive, such as care, protection, love and status.

Catharsis: a term that literally means 'purging'; used in classical psychoanalysis to describe the therapeutic effect of abreaction.

Charisma: a term derived from New Testament Greek meaning the gift of grace; introduced into sociology by Max Weber to describe an 'extraordinary quality' possessed by persons or objects, which is thought to give them unique and magical power.

Collective unconscious: a term introduced by C. G. Jung to designate those aspects of the psyche that are common to all humanity; synonymous with phylogenetic psyche.

Complex: a group or cluster of interconnected ideas and feelings that exert a dynamic effect on conscious experience and on behaviour. Complexes are to the ontogenetic psyche (or personal unconscious) what archetypes are to the phylogenetic psyche (or collective unconscious), the one being dependent on the other in the sense that complexes are 'personations' of archetypes.

Countertransference: the analyst's transference onto the patient.

Delusion: a false belief; characteristic of psychosis.

Ego: the part of the personality that one consciously recognizes as 'I' or 'me'.

Ego-defence mechanism: a mechanism by means of which, according to Freudian theory, the ego defends itself from threats emanating from the id, the superego or the environment. Examples are denial, projection, rationalization, reaction-formation, repression.

Epistemology: study of the basis of knowledge.

Ethology: the study of the behaviour of organisms living in their natural habitats.

Fixation: the process by which libido remains attached to an object appropriate to an earlier state of development. As a result of such fixation, a person will continue to indulge in immature patterns of behaviour, or regress to such behaviour when subjected to stress.

Free association: the patient's response to the basic rule of psychoanalysis to allow every thought to arise and be expressed freely, without censorship or conscious inhibition. When the free flow of associations comes to an end, this is considered to be the result of resistance.

Hallucination: a false sensory perception in the absence of external stimuli; characteristic of psychosis.

Hermeneutics: the art or discipline of interpretation.

Homeostasis: maintenance of balance between opposing mechanisms or systems.

Hysteria: a disorder characterized by the presence of physical symptoms in the absence of any evidence of a physical cause. The symptoms, nevertheless, perform some psychological function that provides the patient with a 'secondary gain'. So-called conversion hysteria presents in a variety of apparent neurological disturbances, such as paralyses, losses of sensation, convulsions and blindness. The condition is encountered much less frequently today than it was in the time of Charcot, Breuer and Freud.

Id: Latin for 'it'; used by Freud's translators for '*das Es*'. 'We approach the id with analogies: we call it a chaos, a cauldron full of seething excitations ... it is filled with energy reaching it from the instincts, but it has no organization, produces no collective will, but only a striving to bring about the satisfaction of instinctual needs subject to the observance of the pleasure-principle' (Freud, 1923).

Individuation: a term used by C. G. Jung to designate the process of personality development that leads to the fullest possible actualization of the archetypal endowment of an individual: 'Individuation means becoming a single, homogeneous being, and, insofar as "individuality" embraces our innermost, last, and incomparable uniqueness, it also implies becoming one's own self. We could therefore translate individuation as "coming to selfhood" or "self-realization" ' (*CW* 7, para. 266).

Lamarckism: the discredited theory originally advanced by the French biologist, Jean-Baptiste Lamarck (1744–1829), which held that experiences acquired by one generation could be transmitted genetically to the next.

Libido: a term used by analysts of all schools to designate a hypothetical form of mental energy. It was originally conceived by Freud as energy derived from the sexual instinct; Jung rejected this as unduly narrow, preferring to conceive libido as general psychic energy that could be expressed in a great variety of forms, of which sexuality was one.

Mandala: Sanskrit word for 'magic circle', a geometric figure incorporating both a circle and a square, divided up into four (or multiples of four) segments radiating from the centre. The mandala stands as a symbol for the wholeness of the Self, the deity and the cosmos.

Natural selection: the principle mechanism of evolutionary change, originally proposed by Darwin (1859). The theory holds that of the range of different individuals making up the population of a given species, those individuals possessing certain advantageous characteristics contribute more offspring to the succeeding generation (that is, they have greater reproductive success than those lacking these characteristics). Provided these advantageous attributes have an inherited basis, they will eventually become established as standard components of the genetic structure of the species (that is, they will be selected by a natural process).

Neurosis: a term dating from the second half of the eighteenth century that originally meant a disease of the nerves; as a result of the work of Charcot and Freud on hysteria towards the end of the nineteenth century, however, neurosis came to be applied precisely to mental disorders that were diseases of the nervous system. Although used less frequently than hitherto, neurosis remains a convenient term for a group of psychiatric disorders that do not involve hallucinations, delusions or loss of insight.

Numinosity: a term introduced into psychology by Jung, who borrowed it from the German theologian Rudolf Otto. Otto used it to describe what he regarded as the fundamental experience common to all religions—namely, the sense of awe and exaltation generated by the feeling of being in the presence of the Creator.

Object: in psychoanalytic parlance, this term is used to refer to a person, or to part of a person, or to a symbol of one or the other.

Object relations: refers to the social need of a subject to establish and maintain a relationship with an object (usually a mother-figure) and later with other significant people in the subject's life. An object relationship may be with an actual person in outer reality or with the mental representation of that person in the subject's psyche.

Objective psyche: Jung sometimes referred to the collective unconscious as the objective psyche in order to stress its co-naturality with all existence: it is as real and as existent as anything in nature. For this reason Jung held that the fundamental natural laws, like the principles of adaptation, homeostasis and growth, apply to the psyche just as surely as to any other biological phenomenon.

Obsessive-compulsive disorder: a fear that things will get out of control and that some catastrophe will ensue; obsessional symptoms and compulsive behaviours arise as quasi-superstitious means to prevent this from happening. Thus patients feel that they 'have got to' think certain thoughts or perform certain acts. Such compulsions can become severely distressing when, as is often the case, they cannot be controlled by voluntary effort.

Oedipus complex: a cluster of largely unconscious ideas and feelings of wishing to possess the parent of the opposite sex and eliminate the parent of the same sex. Freud derived name from the classical Greek story of Oedipus who slayed his father, Laius, and married his mother, Jocasta, without realizing that they were his parents. Freud believed this complex to be universal and phylogenetically determined.

Ontogenetic psyche: those psychic attributes that are dependent for their functional development on the personal history of the individual.

Ontogeny: the development of an organism through the course of its life cycle.

Operant conditioning: learning to perform certain acts which initially occur as random or spontaneous movements through rewards (e.g., food) or punishments (e.g., electric shock).

Paradigm: a term given a technical meaning by T.S. Kuhn in his *The Structure of Scientific Revolutions* (1962). Denying that scientific theories are mere products of induction from sensory experience, Kuhn argued that theories give meaning to facts rather than simply arising out of them. A paradigm is the theoretical framework within which all thinking in a given scientific discipline proceeds. A paradigm shift occurs when one theoretical framework is replaced by another.

Persona: the mask worn by an actor in classical times; Jung used the term to describe the 'packaging' with which we present ourselves to the world. The persona is 'a functional complex that comes into existence for reasons of adaptation or personal convenience, but is by no means identical with the individuality' (*CW* 6, para. 801).

Phylogenetic psyche: those psychic structures and functions that are characteristic of all members of the human species; synonymous with Jung's term 'collective unconscious'.

Phylogeny: the evolutionary origin and development of a species.

Pleasure principle: Freud conceived the psyche in infancy as being motivated entirely by the desire to experience pleasure and avoid pain; only later, when the ego had developed, was the pleasure principle modified by the reality principle. In Freud's view the pleasure principle operated throughout life as a built-in propensity to keep instinctual tensions at a minimal level.

Projection: the unconscious process by which aspects of the self, or feelings or ideas associated with those aspects, are experienced as if they were located in someone or something external to oneself. Projection commonly functions in association with another ego-defence mechanism, denial, in that one denies the existence in oneself of the beliefs, motives or intentions that one attributes to the person, animal or thing on to whom or which one projects them.

Psyche: the totality of all mental processes, unconscious as well as conscious, unlike mind, which is conventionally applied to conscious processes only.

'The psyche is not of today,' wrote Jung; 'its ancestry goes back many millions of years. Individual consciousness is only the flower and the fruit of the season, sprung from the perennial rhizome beneath the earth.' (*CW* 5, p. xxiv).

Psychiatrist: a medically qualified practitioner who specializes in the treatment of mental illness. Only a small minority of psychiatrists are also analysts.

Psychoanalyst: an analyst who subscribes to the theories and who practises the therapeutic techniques devised by Sigmund Freud and developed by his followers. Only a minority of psychoanalysts are medically or psychiatrically qualified.

Psychologist: a pure scientist who studies all behaviour, normal and abnormal, human and animal.

Psychopathology: the study of psychiatric disorders and the provision of theories to account for their existence and development in individuals.

Psychosis: a broad term used to describe those relatively severe psychiatric disorders in which hallucinations and delusions occur in people with relatively poor insight into their condition.

Psychotherapist: a generic term for therapists who use their own minds to treat the minds of others, with or without reference to unconscious processes or using the techniques of any particular school of analysis.

Reality principle: a term used by Freud to designate the environmental constraints imposed on fulfilment of the pleasure principle. Freud believed that the reality principle developed in the course of ontogeny, whereas the pleasure principle was innate and present at birth.

REM sleep: rapid eye-movement sleep, which at regular intervals during the night is reliably associated with the experience of dreams and with characteristic physiological changes in the body of the dreamer.

Repression: the ego-defence mechanism by which an unacceptable impulse or idea is rendered unconscious.

Resistance: a term introduced by Freud to account for the unwillingness of his patients to accept his interpretations—an unwillingness he invariably attributed to their reluctance to face the unpleasant nature of their unconscious wishes rather than to the possibility that his interpretations could be wrong.

Schizoid personality: a type of personality structure characterized by a reluctance to enter into close personal relationships, a preference for solitary activities, and displaying a marked degree of emotional detachment.

Self: a term introduced by Jung for the dynamic nucleus of the core of the personality responsible for the process of individuation: the Self incorporates the entire archetypal potential of the unconscious psyche.

Separation anxiety: anxiety experienced at the prospect of becoming separated from a person to whom a bond of attachment has been formed.

Shadow: Jung's term for the aspect of the Self which remains unconscious because it is repressed by the superego, or unactivated because of deficiencies in the life experience of the individual.

Sociobiology: a term introduced by E. O. Wilson for his approach to the study of behaviour; it is based on the assumption that the survival of the gene ultimately determines the form of the behaviour studied.

Superego: a term originally introduced by Freud which has come to designate that inner moral authority or ethical complex that monitors individual behaviour in such a way as to make it acceptable first to the parents and later to society.

Transcendent function: Jung's term for the mutual influence which is exerted between the ego and the Self in the course of personality development and individuation.

Transference: the process whereby a patient transfers on to the person of the analyst feelings, anticipations and notions, which derive from important figures related to in the past. Freud came to view transference as an essential part of the therapeutic process. By remaining detached, and declining to fulfil the patient's anticipations, the analyst seeks to create a novel situation through which it may be possible to interpret to the patient that he or she is behaving as if the analyst were his or her father, mother, grandparent, sibling, etc. This transference relationship is to be distinguished from the analytic relationship (which refers to the total relationship, both conscious and unconscious, between analyst and patient) and the therapeutic alliance (which refers to their collaborative effort to confront and resolve the problems that brought the patient into analysis).

BIBLIOGRAPHY

Arlow, J. A. (1982). 'Psychoanalaytic Education: A psychoanalytic perspective', *Annual of Psychoanalysis*, 10: 5–20.

Bennet, E. A. (1982). *Meetings with Jung*. Anchor, London.

Crews, Frederick. (1993) 'The Unknown Freud', *New York Review of Books*, 18 November, pp. 55–66 .

_____. (1994). 'The Revenge of the Repressed', *New York Review of Books*, Part I, 17 November, pp. 54–60; Part II, 1 December, pp. 49–58.

Dawes, Robyn, M. (1994). *House of Cards: Psychology and Psychotherapy Built on Myth*. The Free Press, New York and London.

Diamond, Jared. (1991). *The Rise and Fall of the Third Chimpanzee*. Vintage, London.

Ellenberger, Henri. (1970). *The Discovery of the Unconscious*. Basic Books, New York.

_____. (1993). *Beyond the Unconscious: Essays of Henri F. Ellenberger,* in *The History of Psychiatry*, ed. Mark S. Micale. Princeton University Press, Princeton, NJ.

Erikson, E. H. (1962). *Young Man Luther: A Study in Psychoanalysis & History*. Norton, New York.

Esterson, Allen. (1993). *Seductive Mirage: An Exploration of the Work of Sigmund Freud*. Open Court, Chicago, IL.

Eysenck, H. J. (1952). 'The Effects of Psychotherapy: An evaluation', *Journal of Consulting Psychology*, 16: 319-24.

Ferenczi, Sándor. (1995). *The Clinical Diary of Sándor Ferenczi*, ed. Judith Dupont; trans. Michael Balint and Nicola Zarday Jackson. Harvard University Press, Cambridge, MA.

Freud, Sigmund. (1953–74). *The Standard Edition of the Complete Psychological Works of Sigmund Freud*, ed. James Strachey, The Hogarth Press and The Institute of Psycho-Analysis, London. Sources of quotations from *The Standard Edition* are indicated by (*SE*) followed by the volume number followed by the page number from which the quotation is taken (e.g., *SE* 2, p. 44).

_____. (1893–95). *Studies on Hysteria* (Vol. 2).

_____. (1900). *The Interpretation of Dreams* (Vols. 4 and 5). Penguin, 1976.

_____. (1910). *Five Lectures on Psycho-Analysis* (Vol. 11).

_____. (1913). *Totem and Taboo* (Vol. 13).

_____. (1920). *Beyond the Pleasure Principle* (Vol. 18).

_____. (1923). *The Ego and the Id* (Vol. 19).

_____. (1925). *An Autobiographical Study* (Vol. 20).

_____. (1933). *New Introductory Lectures on Psychoanalysis* (Vol. 22).

_____. (1927). *The Future of an Illusion* (Vol. 21).

_____. (1930). *Civilization and its Discontents* (Vol. 21).

_____. (1937). *Analysis Terminable and Interminable* (Vol. 23)

_____. (1939). *Moses and Monotheism* (Vol. 23).

_____. (1940). *An Outline of Psycho-Analysis* (Vol. 23).

_____. (1974). *The Freud/Jung Letters*, see McGuire, William (ed.).

_____. (1985). 'The Freud/Fliess Letters', see Masson, Jeffrey, ed.

Frosh, Stephen. (1998*). For and Against Psychoanalysis*. Routledge, London.

Gay, Peter. (1988). *Freud: A Life For Our Time.* J. M. Dent & Sons, London
and Melbourne.

Hobson, J. Allan. (1988). *The Dreaming Brain*. Basic Books, New York.

Jones, Ernest. (1953–57). *Sigmund Freud: Life and Work* (3 vols). The Hogarth
Press, London.

Jung, C. G. The majority of quotations in the text are taken either from *The Collected Works of C. G. Jung* (1953–78); ed. H. Read, M. Fordham and G. Adler, and published in London by Routledge, in New York by Pantheon Books
(1953–60) and the Bollingen Foundation (1961–67), and in Princeton, NJ, by
Princeton University Press (1967–78); or from *Memories, Dreams, Reflections* (1963), published in London by Routledge & Kegan Paul, and in New
York by Random House. Sources of quotations from *The Collected Works*
are indicated by the volume number followed by the number of the paragraph
from which the quotation is taken (e.g., *CW* 10, para. 441). Quotations from
Memories, Dreams, Reflections are indicated by the page number thus: *MDR*,
p. 111.

_____. (1906). *The Psychology of Dementia Praecox*: originally published in
German, now available in English (*CW* 3) published in 1960.

_____. (1911–12). *Transformations and Symbols of the Libido*: originally
published in German, now available in English as *Symbols of Transformation*
(*CW* 5) published in 1956.

_____. (1921). *Psychological Types*: originally published in German, now available in English as *Psychological Types* (*CW* 6) published in 1971.

_____. (1933). *Modern Man in Search of a Soul*. Kegan Paul, London.

_____. (2009). *The Red Book* (Liber Novum). The Philemon Foundation and W. W. Norton, New York.

Krafft-Ebing, R. von. (1965). *Psychopathia Sexualis:* originally published in 1886; Stein & Day, New York.

Kuhn, T. S. (1962). *The Structure of Scientific Revolutions*. University of Chicago Press, Chicago, IL.

Lakoff, R. T., and Coyne, J. C. (1993). *Father Knows Best: The Use and Abuse of Power in Freud's Case of "Dora"*. Teachers College Press, New York.

Macmillan, Malcolm. (1997). *Freud Evaluated: The Completed Arc*. The MIT Press, Cambridge, MA.

Masson, Jeffrey. (1984). *The Assault on Truth: Freud's Suppression of the Seduction Theory*. Farrar, Straus & Giroux Inc., New York; (1992) reissued with a new preface as *The Assault on Truth: Freud and Child Sexual Abuse*, HarperCollins.

_____. (1988, revised 1990). *Against Therapy: Emotional Tyranny and the Myth of Psychological Healing*: revised edition, Fontana, London.

Masson, Jeffrey (ed.). (1985). *The Complete Letters of Sigmund Freud to Wilhelm Fliess 1887–1904*. Harvard University Press, Cambridge, MA.

McGuire, William (ed.). (1974). *The Freud/Jung Letters: The Correspondence Between Sigmund Freud and C. G. Jung*, trans. Ralph Manheim and R. F. C. Hull, Princeton University Press, Princeton, NJ.

McGuire, William, and Hull, R. F. C. (1977). *C.G. Jung Speaking*. Princeton University Press, Princeton, NJ.

Medawar, P.B. (1975). 'Review of Irving S. Cooper's The *Victim is Always the Same'*, *New York Review of Books*, 23 January.

Nietzsche, F. (1956). *The Genealogy of Morals, An Attack*: originally published in 1887; ed. Francis Golffing. Anchor, New York.

Noll, Richard. (1994). *The Jung Cult: Origins of a Charismatic Movement*. Princeton University Press, Princeton, NJ.

_____. (1997). *The Aryan Christ: The Secret Life of Carl Jung*. Random House, New York.

Parry, G. (1966). *NHS Psychotherapy Services in England*. NH Executive, 135–155. Waterloo Road, London.

Roazen, Paul. (1992). *Freud and His Followers*. Da Capo Press, New York.

Roth, A., and Fonagy, Peter. (1996; second edition, 2005). *What Works For Whom? A Critical Review of Psychotherapy Research*. The Guilford Press, New York.

Ryle, Anthony. (1990). *Cognitive Analytic Therapy: Active Participation in Change*. John Wiley & Sons, Chichester, UK.

Schopenhauer, Arthur. (1995). *The World as Will and Idea:* originally published 1819; trans. Jill Berman. Everyman, London.

Stevens, Anthony. (1982). *Archetype: A Natural History of the Self*. Routledge & Kegan Paul, London, and William Morrow & Co., New York. New and revised edition: (2002) *Archetype Revisited: An Updated Natural History of the Self*. Brunner-Routledge, London; (2003) Inner City Books, Toronto.

_____. (1991). *On Jung*. Penguin, London.

Stevens, Anthony, and Price, John. (1996). *Evolutionary Psychiatry: A New Beginning*. Routledge, London.

Storr, Anthony. (1996). *Feet of Clay: A Study of Gurus*. HarperCollins, London.

Sulloway, Frank, J. (1979). *Freud, Biologist of the Mind: Beyond the Psycho-analytic Legend*. Burnett Books/Andre Deutsch, London.

_____. (1991). 'Reassessing Freud's Case Histories. The social construction of psychoanalysis', *Isis*, Vol. 82: 245–75. London.

Webster, Richard. (1995). *Why Freud Was Wrong: Sin, Science and Psycho-analysis*. HarperCollins, London.

Wenegrat, Brant. (1984). *Sociobiology and Mental Disorder: A New View*. Addison Wesley, Menlo Park, CA.

Westen, D., Novotny, C. A., and Thompson-Brenner, H. (2004). 'The Empirical Status of Empirically Supported Psychotherapies: Assumptions, findings, and reporting in controlled clinical trials', *Psychological Bulletin*, 130(4): 631–3.

Wilcocks, Robert. (1994). *Maelzel's Chess Player: Sigmund Freud and the Rhetoric of Deceit*. Rowman and Littlefield, Lanham, MD.

INDEX

Jung, C. G. *(cont.)*
    grounds psychology in biology,
        91-92
    guru, 82, 85, 87, 106
    interest in alchemy, 85, 102-103
    psychology as a 'subjective
        confession', 90-91, 107
    President of the International
        Psychoanalytic Association,
        75, 80
    Red Book, The 82
    relations with father, 83-84
        with Freud, 75-81
        with mother, 83
    schizoid personality, 84-85
    two personalities, 85
Jungfrauen, 82
Jungian analysis, 101-109. *See
    also* analytical psychology
    differences from Freudian
        analysis summarized, 108-
        109
    four stages of, 101-102
    importance of feeling in, 107
    techniques of, 103-104

Kant, Immanuel, 63
Kleinian analysis, 58, 107
Klein, Melanie (neé Reizes), 90
Koller, Carl, 34
Krafft-Ebing, Richard von, 48, 65,
    70, 91
Kreuzlingen Sanatorium, 37

Lakoff, Robin T., 26, 56
La Rochefoucauld, 64
Learning theory, 22
libido, 50, 76, 79, 80
    fixation of, 51
liberation philosophy, 72
Liber Novum. See *Red Book, The*
life cycle, 23, 94, 100
Logos principle, 87
Macmillan, Malcolm, 27, 65

mandala, 89
Maslow, Abraham, 23
Masson, Jeffrey, 26, 41, 49
masturbation, 42, 47, 55
Maudsley Hospital, 22
Medawar, Sir Peter, 26
Meynert, Theodor, 33, 34, 81
Modern Man in Search of a Soul,
    31
Moses and Monotheism, 40

'nasal reflex neurosis', 46, 49
NHS (British National Health
    Service), 21, 24
'Neurasthenia', 42, 45
neurosis, 42-43, 45, 60, 76, 101
    as form of adaptation, 99
    Freud's theory of, 35-45, 51, 56
    actual neurosis, 42
    'general neurosis of the age',
        100
    neurotica, 42
    psychoneurosis, 42
Nietzsche, Friedrich, 23, 63-64, 88
Nirvana principle, 50
Noll, Richard, 27, 75, 88

Obholzer, Karin, 56
objective psyche, 92, 102
object relations theory, 26, 67
obsessive-compulsive disorder, 22,
    42, 45, 56
Occham's razor, 45
Oedipus complex, 53-54, 69, 80
On Jung, 27
Outline of Pyschoanalysis, 60

Papini, Giovanni, 66
Parry, G., 20
pathogenic secret, 36
Pauli, Wolfgang, 108
Perls, Fritz, 23
persona, 92
personal equation, 107

Philemon, 87
phylogenetic psyche, 75, 89, 96. *See also* collective unconscious
phylogeny, 109
placebo effect, 32
pleasure principle, 64
Preiswerk, Hélène, 85-87
Price, John, 67
primal scene, 55-57
primary process thinking, 64
'primordial images', 80, 95. *See also* archetypes
'Project for a Scientific Psychology', 44, 50
projection, 90
projective identification, 102
psyche, 75
    as organ of adaptation, 92-93
    self-healing capacity of, 93
    as self-regulatory system, 92-93
    See also objective psyche; phylogenetic psyche
psychiatry, 19. *See also* evolutionary psychiatry
psychic inertia, 60
psychoanalysis, 9, 19, 30-74
    basic concepts of, 38-39
    'basic rule' of, 38
    Freud's first mention of, 18
    impact on Western culture, 25, 70-74
    number of sessions per week, 21
    present status of, 25-29
psychobiology, 44
psychodrama, 23
psychodynamic therapy, 21, 28
Psychological Types, 82, 90
psychology, 19, 22. *See also* evolutionary psychology; Jungian analysis
Psychology of Dementia Praecox, The, 75-76
'primal scene', 55

psychosis, 81
psychotherapy, 19-29
    as an art, 103
Rank, Otto, 70
reality principle, 64
'Recommendations to Physicians Practising Psycho-Analysis', 58
'recovered memory syndrome', 41, 72
Red Book, The, 82
Reich, Wilhelm, 81
Reik, Theodor, 68
REM sleep, 49
repression, 38-40, 67
research, 9-10
    Dodo bird verdict, 10
resistance 38-40, 79, 90
Roazen, Paul, 68, 90, 109
Rogers, Carl, 23
Roth, A., 20
Ryle, Anthony, 25

Sachs, Hans, 68, 70
Salome, 87-88
Salpétrière Hospital, 34
schizoid personality, 66, 84-85
schizophrenia, 78-79, 82
Schopenhauer, Arthur, 62-63
secondary process thinking, 64
Self, the, 85, 89, 92
self-healing, 93
sex, as aetiological factor, 68, 76
sexual seduction, 41-43
sexual symbolism, 52-53
sexual theory, 43-46, 76
sexual trauma, 40-43, 72
sexuality, infantile, 43, 51-52
shadow, 92, 101
shaman, 82, 106
Silberer, Herbert, 81
Society of Analytical Psychology (SAP), 21
soul, loss of, 3, 100
Standard Social Science Model, 95

126

Also by Anthony Stevens in this Series

Title 105. *ARCHETYPE REVISITED: An Updated Natural History of the Self*

ISBN 1-894574-06-0. Illustrated. Index. 416 pp. 2003. $50

C. G. Jung's concept of the archetypes of the collective unconscious has traditionally been the property of analyticall psychology and at times dismissed as "mystical" by scientists. But Jung himself described archetypes as biological entities which must be amenable to empirical study.

In *Archetype: A Natural History of the Self* (1982), Anthony Stevens presented the key to opening up a scientific approach to the archetypes. At last, in a creative leap made possible by the cross-fertilization of several specialist disciplines, psychiatry was integrated with analytical psychology, biology and the social sciences. The result is an immensely enriched science of human behavior.

This revised and greatly expanded edition of Dr. Stevens' groundbreaking book further explores the connections between the archetypes and other fields of study such as ethology and sociobiology, resulting in the new discipline called evolutionary psychotherapy.

Anthony Stevens, M.D., worked in England as a Jungian analyst and psychiatrist for over 30 years. He is the author of several other books, including *On Jung* (1990) and, with John Price, *Evolutionary Psychiatry: A New Beginning* (2000). He now lives on the island of Corfu, Greece.

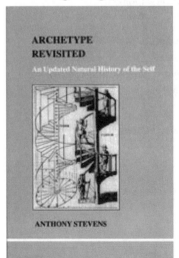

"I recommend Dr. Stevens' book as one of the best introductions to Jung's thought and its practical applications."
—*Dr. Anthony Storr, Times Literary Supplement, England..*

"Dr. Anthony Stevens has made a major contribution to Jungian studies, as well as indicating the common ground between seemingly incompatible disciplines."
—*British Medical Journal.*

Studies in Jungian Psychology
by Jungian Analysts

Quality Paperbacks

Prices and payment in $US (except in Canada and Visa orders, $Cdn)

Bees, Honey and the Hive: Circumambulating the Centre.
Frith Luton (Melbourne) ISBN 978-1-894574-32-7. 208 pp. $30

Risky Business: Environmental Disasters and the Nature Archetype
Stephen Foster (Boulder, CO) ISBN 978-0-919123-33-4. 128 pp. $25

Miles To Go Before I Sleep: Growing Up Puer (a Jungian Romance)
Daryl Sharp (Toronto) 978-1-894574-36-5 128 pp. $25

Clinical Chaos: The Strange Attractors of Childhood Trauma.
John R. Van Eenwyk (Olympia, WA) ISBN 978-1-894574-37-2. 192 pp. $30.

The Sacred Psyche: A Psychological Approach to the Psalms
Edward F. Edinger (Los Angeles) ISBN 978-1-894574-09-9. 160 pp. $25

Eros and Pathos: Shades of Love and Suffering
Aldo Carotenuto (Rome) ISBN 978- 0-919123-39-7. 144 pp. $25

Descent to the Goddess: A Way of Initiation for Women
Sylvia Brinton Perera (New York) ISBN 978-0-919123-05-2. 112 pp. $25

The Illness That We Are: A Jungian Critique of Christianity
John P. Dourley (Ottawa) ISBN 978-0-919123-16-8. 128 pp. $25

Coming To Age: The Croning Years and Late-Life Transformation
Jane R. Prétat (Providence) ISBN 978-0-919123-63-2. 144 pp. $25

Jungian Dream Interpretation: A Handbook of Theory and Practice
James A. Hall, M.D. (Dallas) ISBN 978-0-919123-12-0. 128 pp. $25

Phallos: Sacred Image of the Masculine
Eugene Monick (Scranton) ISBN 978-0-919123-26-7. 30 illustrations. 144 pp. $25

The Sacred Prostitute: Eternal Aspect of the Feminine
Nancy Qualls-Corbett (Birmingham) ISBN 978-0-919123-31-1. Illustrated. 176 pp. $30

Jung Uncorked: Rare Vintages from the Cellar of Analytical Psychology
Three vols. *Daryl Sharp (Toronto)* ISBN 978-1-894574-21-1/22-8/24-2. 128 pp. $25 each

The Pregnant Virgin: A Process of Psychological Development
Marion Woodman (Toronto) ISBN 978-0-919123-20-5. Illustrated. 208 pp. $30pb/$35hc

Discounts: any 1-9 books, 20%; 10-19, 25%; 20 or more, 40% .

Add Postage/Handling: 1-2 books, $6 surface ($10 air); 3-4 books, $12 surface
($16 air); 5-9 books, $16 surface ($25 air); 10 or more, $16 surface ($30 air)

Visa credit cards accepted. Toll-free: Tel. 1-888-927-0355; Fax 1-888=924-1814.

INNER CITY BOOKS, Box 1271, Station Q, Toronto, ON M4T 2P4, Canada
Tel. (416) 927-0355 / Fax (416) 924-1814 / booksales@innercitybooks.net